God Hates Abuse

Abuse and the Doctrine of Headship and Submission

Robin Mullins Senger

Copyright © 2016 Robin Mullins Senger

All Scripture quotations, unless otherwise indicated, are taken from The Holy Bible, New Revised Standard Version Bible, copyright © 1989 the Division of Christian Education of the National Council of the Churches of Christ in the United States of America. Used by permission. All rights reserved. Scripture quotations marked (AMP) are taken from the Amplified Bible, copyright © 1987 All rights reserved.

Cover design by SelfPubBookCovers.com/BeeJavier

This book provides limited information on faith, domestic violence and abuse, and relevant stories from my life. I have made every effort to be as accurate as possible. Conversations and recollections come from my perspective and memory and are retold in a way that evokes the feeling and meaning of what was said and done. In all instances, the essence of dialogue is accurate. Names and identities have been changed.

I do not offer legal or other professional advice. Please seek appropriate expertise from professionals such as law enforcement, legal counsel, safe houses, advocacy and other services as applicable. Readers should take full responsibility for their safety and know their limits.

Links and websites in this book are provided for informational purposes only and do not constitute endorsement of all content or any products or services provided by these websites. The links and websites are subject to change, expire, or redirect without any notice.

Dedication

For my Sky-Bird, my Joy-Bird, and my Song-Bird, who inspire me every day to live free and sing loud. And for Kyle, who helped me become who I wanted and needed to be. May we never stop laughing together!

Table of Contents

Preface 1
Introduction 5
Chapter One: Defining the Difference between Abusive and Challenging 14
   1. The Abuser Defined 14
   2. But He's Mostly Good! 18
   3. Isolation is Dangerous 20
   4. Where Is Your Marriage on This Scale? 22
   5. Is His Fruit Good or Toxic? 24
   6. Toxic and a Fool 29
   7. He Says "Judge Not!" 30
   8. Be Cautious of Testimonies 32
   9. A Final Question 35
Chapter Two: How to Rightly Interpret Scripture 37
   1. Conflict between My Heart and My Head 37
   2. Why You Should Read the Bible for Yourself 38
   3. Six Principles for Discernment 40
Chapter Three: Headship and Submission in a Christian Marriage 45
Chapter Four: Escaping the Ultimate Loneliness 63
   1. Abandonment 74
   2. Adultery 75
   3. Lust 79
   4. Idolatry 80
   5. Physical and Sexual Abuse 81
   6. Fraud 81
   7. Fear for Your Life 82
   8. Passive Neglect 83
Chapter Five: Options 86
   1. Staying 86
   2. Separating 93
   3. Counseling or Mediation 95
   4. Turning to the Church for Help 96
   5. Divorce 104
Chapter Six: A Christian Wife's Biblical Response to Abuse 109
   1. Response to His Abuse 111
   2. Response to People Blaming You 118
   3. Response to His Claimed Repentance (signs it's authentic) 119

    4. Grief 123
    5. Forgiveness 126
Chapter Seven: Freedom from Fear 131
Appendix A: Scriptures for Prayer and Meditation 138
    Children 138
    Purity 140
    Harmony 141
    Rebellion 142
    Parenting 142
    Victory 143
    Protection 144
    Provision 145
    Healing 146
    Courage 146
    Peace 147
Appendix B: Warning Signs of Abuse 148
Appendix C: Risk Assessment 150
Appendix D: Safety Plan 152
Appendix E: Safety-Packing Checklist 155
Appendix F: Technology Safety 157
Works Cited 160
Resources 165
    Helplines (accessed January 2016) 165
    Websites (accessed January 2016) 166
    Articles (accessed January 2016) 167
    Recommended Books 168
About the Author 170
Connect with Robin 171

Preface

God Hates Abuse is a book of hope for Christian wives caught in the web of spousal abuse and violence.

This book grew out of my journey of recovery and healing from a dangerous and abusive marriage. My husband Brian (not his real name) believed God gave him the right to rule over his family in any way that pleased him. It was after I fled with our children that I began doing extensive research to find out if there was any biblical justification for my decision to leave. What I discovered shattered a spiritual paradigm of unquestioned male superiority and along with it my guilt for not "submitting" to my husband's spiritual headship.

I blogged about my journey in finding acceptance, comfort and peace from the Bible in the face of spousal abuse. Sharing my journey online was therapeutic, although I did not really expect anyone to read it. Surprisingly, my story resonated with thousands of readers who shared similar feelings of confusion over perceived biblical laws of headship and submission. None of these perceptions was compassionate toward them as victims of spiritual, emotional, psychological, economic, legal and physical abuse by their husbands.

While still in my marriage, I could not find the help I needed to resolve my spiritual conflict. Since I was closely monitored, I had to be cautious of anything that might tip off Brian that I was anything less than grateful and thrilled with him. Careful to erase my history on the computer, I searched often for spiritual guidance in an abusive marriage, but only found a plethora of websites telling me to submit or burn. They added to my guilt and misery rather than offering anything helpful. It wasn't that I wanted a divorce. I just wanted to survive my marriage with some modicum of internal peace. In the end, I fled out of desperation to protect my children.

From the safety of our new home, I delved into the spiritual implications of what I had just done. To my great surprise and relief, I learned that I had not committed some unforgivable sin. I was not inferior, worthless, stupid, crazy or selfish. Best of all, I had actually done something that pleased God and was aligned with his purpose. My relationship with God began to flourish and my children thrived.

Even though starting over was extremely hard, God helped us every step of the way.

This book does not condone and encourage divorce for every unhappy marriage. I am primarily offering insight for Christian women who find themselves in a dangerous and destructive marriage, and believe they have no alternative but to submit to violence and abuse.

Victims often struggle with deciphering between love, immaturity, ignorance and the truly abusive. It is confusing when there are many dynamics and emotions involved. Still, there are clear biblical guidelines to help bring clarity to each individual situation. I conformed to Brian's biblical interpretation out of fear of him and uncertainty about God's expectations. As time went by, I often questioned my sanity and value. Reality was a mixed up, confusing and painful mess. Even though I had been professionally trained as an advocate in domestic violence, pinning down the signs of it in my own marriage was extraordinarily difficult. My desire to please God added to the guilt and weight of it all.

As I hope to prove to you in this book, faith in God is not misplaced and he is not condemning those who suffer under the oppression of abuse. God used my marriage to Brian to teach me the truth about who he is, and what he wants for women who find themselves trapped in heart-breaking relationships. Coming into the knowledge of biblical truth allowed inner healing and personal growth that stopped the cycle of abuse. It opened the door to an amazing life full of peace and joy and being able to walk in his purpose for my life. I can say now that it was all worth it - every bit of pain and heartache was worth it to be able to experience the life I now enjoy with my precious daughters.

I want to make clear up front that I am not a theologian, and do not pretend to be. I bring years of experience from the trenches of my own painful relationships and helping others through theirs. I greatly value my professional experience as an advocate, and currently enjoy being a life coach for people experiencing abusive or dysfunctional relationships with anyone.

Rather than offer my own biblical interpretations, this book leans heavily on the expertise of trained pastors and other religious leaders. What I learned from them helped me tremendously in making sense of what I had experienced, and I want to share it in hopes it will help you too. For brevity, I only quote what I feel is particularly useful, especially because you may be in a crisis and not have the freedom or time for deeper research. Get the books, visit the websites, and delve deeper into their work as you can.

Most importantly, read the Bible for yourself. Study it. Take the information in this book and line it up with your own study of the Bible. 1 Thessalonians 5:21 admonishes us to "test everything; hold fast to what is good." Begin a private conversation with God about everything that weighs on you. Ultimately, you must follow what he reveals to you in his Word and how he leads you. He will never fail you in this.

My goal is to perhaps open a new window of thought, shift the paradigm a bit, and start you on your own journey of self-discovery and renewed faith and hope.

This book would not be possible without those special people willing to walk with me at a time of personal risk and the inevitable messiness that accompanies domestic abuse.

The primary weapon abusers use is isolation and secrecy. I will never forget the first time I reached out for help. I didn't tell the person everything at the time. I just wanted to see what the reaction would be to a little bit of what was happening, and I mostly wanted to see if the other person thought I was as crazy as I felt. The response was compassionate and emboldened me to speak up more. With the support of a half dozen people, I gained the courage and strength to flee. At our new home, I encountered more people brave enough to walk with me through a difficult divorce and recovery.

For the privacy of these people, I will not list their names here, but they know who they are. I will always be thankful to them for picking me up when I fell down, believing in me when I didn't believe in myself, and inspiring me to be more than I ever dreamed I could be. Some of them were in and out of my life briefly, but their kindness will never be forgotten. A few of them have been with me for the long haul and have proven to be true friends and mentors of tremendous value and worth. I love them dearly!

Each day in the United States an average of three women and one man are murdered by their intimate partner (statisticbrain.com). Between four and five children die daily from child abuse and neglect. More than 80% of these child maltreatment fatalities involve at least one parent as perpetrator (childhelp.org). Abuse to the point of death for women and children is so common that it doesn't make the news unless the people involved have celebrity status. Many of these statistics are Christian wives, hoping their husband would learn to love them and their children if they just prayed harder and submitted more. Or that God would miraculously change him. God has already given women ample concessions for leaving abuse, and he promises to help them through whatever difficulties are encountered.

This book will empower Christian wives with spiritual knowledge to respond to abuse in the best way possible for them. Peace with God, combined with community resources and support, is a set-up for a better life free from abuse. Violence is NOT God's will for anyone. Victims can live free of guilt, shame, and feeling like a hypocrite if they do leave their abuser, or even if they choose to stay.

It is my hope that God's overflowing heart of love for the oppressed and victimized will be revealed in this book, and that victims will find hope, clarity and renewed faith for courageous living!

Introduction

A few years ago, I was in a dangerous, toxic "Christian" marriage and couldn't take it anymore! Very frightened of leaving my husband Brian, I believed that if I stayed I would possibly be dead by his initiative within a year. At least that was what people who knew him better than I warned me of. My close circle of confidants feared I would be the victim of a fatal "accident" by my husband. The police called me frequently to see if I was okay, since I was too scared to file for a restraining order.

In time, I also had an additional worry. Word got to me that men, newly released from prison, were looking for Brian to settle a score since he had ratted on them, causing their incarceration. I worried about what would happen if they showed up at our isolated farm, especially since Brian was increasingly sporadic coming home. Would they hurt the children or me to send a message to Brian? I started composing a letter to be found in the event I was murdered, feeling as if I was crazy to even be writing it.

After months of agonizing over whether to stay or leave, a sickening discovery one morning prompted a final decision to flee. I loaded into my car some clothes, my mom's paintings, my three young daughters and their kittens, and a pet chicken named Lily. We drove across the country to my parents' home, hoping and praying for a better life.

If you are reading this book, it is likely that you are experiencing your own heart-breaking relationship. You probably identify as a Christian. Your spouse may also consider himself a Christian and justify his behavior with Bible verses. While deciding whether to stay or leave a painful relationship is hard for anyone, deeply ingrained, faulty religious beliefs compound a Christian victim's ability to get away from an abuser. It was a big issue I struggled with. I was more afraid of disobeying God than I was of being murdered.

Do you identify with that feeling? Most Christian wives do. Our devotion to God and family is so strong, that we will endure any hardship to keep heaven smiling upon us. The one thing that finally overrode my fear was the frightening realization of what would happen to my children if I weren't there to protect them. I decided that I loved my children too much to subject them to inevitable danger and abuse. I decided that if God's wrath was to fall on me for no longer submitting to my husband's headship, well then, fall it must... I just had to protect my daughters.

It was after I fled that God was able to help me see the truth about him, and that he had never wanted me or the children to stay in that dangerous situation. I had stayed far longer than I ever needed to. Thankfully, I did find the courage to leave when I did, and God lovingly guided us through the difficult days ahead.

Let me give you a little of my background. I was raised in a loving Christian home on a small farm in dry eastern Oregon. Our community economy was primarily agriculture, timber and livestock. We had one flashing streetlight in town. My dad was a carpenter and my mom a homemaker. Since my siblings were at least 12 years older, I grew up mostly alone. I enjoyed playing with my stuffed animals and pets, climbing the haystack, playing in the barn and sneaking through the tall wheat that grew on our farm. I loved it when dad's Hereford cows started calving, because it inevitably meant some mama in the middle of the night would need dad to help turn her calf properly and pull it out. If I was lucky, a baby would need to be bottle fed for a while. Life couldn't get any better when mom and dad got me my own horse - it was instant inseparable love and friendship.

I suppose that growing up with minimal media and friends helped me develop a close relationship with God. I considered him my best friend and spent hours talking to him. I felt close to him and loved. After leaving home, I developed a habit of getting up early and fixing both him and myself a cup of hot chocolate. I would sit and read my Bible and talk to him as I had always done. Sometimes if I decided to not get up and just sleep, I would feel him tug at my heart as if to say, *Robin, get up! This is OUR time together!* The intense love I felt from him, and the knowledge that he enjoyed these quiet times together as much as I, always put a smile on my face and I gladly got up and poured us a cup of hot chocolate. These times of intimacy carried me through many dark days ahead - days I couldn't fathom would happen to me.

One day, a friend asked me to volunteer at the local women and children's crisis center. They were in need of extra help, and since I had time, would I please consider it? I said no. I had no experience with domestic violence and abuse and was sure I would not fit in or like it. I wanted to do other things with my life, but any door I tried to open seemed bolted shut. My friend continued to ask me for help and I finally went in just to get her to stop bugging me. I didn't realize it at the time, but God was directing my steps. This would become my life's work and passion.

Unfortunately, I was also attracted to the wrong kind of men. I learned all about the red flags of abusers and should have been able to avoid them, but couldn't. I continued life stuck in my own endless and painful cycle of toxic relationships, while helping others get free of theirs.

For me, the hardest part of working at the crisis center was that I didn't know how to help our toughest clients - Christian wives. These women stayed with, or temporarily left before going back to their abusive husbands, because they unwaveringly believed God required them to do so. They thought they had to stay, submit and pray quietly for their husbands.

Sometimes our shelter referred inquiring Christian clients to a local pastor who had offered to serve these women. What we didn't realize was that some pastors would counsel the women to go back home and submit to their husbands per traditional religious teachings. I'm sure their intentions were good, but the result was bitter for these wives and their children.

I was, and am, a committed Christian myself. I wanted to please God, to be obedient to his Word, and to do the right thing for everyone involved. Like most others, I only knew the traditional church's teachings on wifely submission. I didn't know any other way. So the cycle for all of us continued. Eventually I felt disillusioned and burned out, and I ventured into the seemingly safe and fun world of Christian online dating.

I met Brian on an online Christian singles-dating site. I was attracted to his passionate relationship with God and traditional beliefs. Even though he had a shady past, his testimony of God's intervention and deliverance was truly miraculous and inspiring. Accustomed to hearing life-changing testimonies in church, it never occurred to me that Brian's testimony might not be authentic.

Brian seemed to know exactly how to appeal to my deeply spiritual side, and challenged me to go deeper in my faith. I loved the intense Bible studies and prayer times we had, and I admired his grasp of the "deep" things of spiritual life. Ready to be a full-time mother and homemaker, I thought I had found an incredibly good man and leader for our household. I thought I was finally leaving toxic relationships behind me forever.

Our story started out romantic and idealistic. It seemed so perfect that we married within a couple months of meeting each other. But a few years later, as I shared previously, I was fleeing from him for my life. God didn't make me marry this guy, and in hindsight, I feel he tried to warn me against it. However, God stayed faithful to the children and I through the next few tumultuous years.

Since I didn't take the time to get to know Brian before marrying him, I got to know him afterwards. He had strange ideas such as wanting to move every three months. Brian also talked to a "guardian angel" called "Paul" and did whatever "Paul" told him to do regardless of my concerns. Brian would also feel undervalued at a job and quit on a whim. Whatever Brian did or said always had a deeply spiritual motive and value to it. This included isolating me from family and friends because he believed they would try to break us up. He trusted no one, and respected no one other than his grandfather - the very person who had introduced him to drugs and violence at a young age.

When I would question something, Brian would pityingly show me how "religious" and in error I was, and how I needed to come to his side and be truly "spiritual." He patiently took the time to show me from the Bible the fallacy of my thinking and ways. He believed that since he was the head of the family, it was his responsibility to guide me in all things and I had to submit to it.

Privately, I figured it was better to just let Brian (and "Paul") do what they were going to do, since it didn't interfere with my being a happy full-time mom. I was supremely content raising our two daughters, and as long as nothing took me away from them, I didn't worry too much about anything else. Brian was strange, but he provided for our needs. I thought life was good.

However, I was naive. In hindsight, I should have been VERY worried. Immediately following the birth of our third daughter, Brian gave up the Christian facade he had been using. I think he felt secure that I was dependent on him financially and was a mild-mannered, mostly submissive, Christian wife. I wasn't going anywhere. The change in him progressed into a predictable cycle. I would be hurt over some new behavior and make the necessary mental, emotional, and spiritual adjustments to cope, and hope that was the last of it.

Within a year, Brian's thinking and behavior had reached a dangerous point. When our daughters were just four, three, and barely one year old, Brian impulsively took us to South America because "Paul" told him to. Brian assured me that he had everything planned out and it would be a great adventure. He had the funds to tide us over until he picked up work in construction or at a mission.

True, I had always seen him able to get work seemingly without much effort in a new place. Charm was his trademark and it got him pretty much anything he wanted. My gut told me though that this was not a good idea, and when I would cautiously start to share my concerns, Brian would turn dark and angry. I was afraid to do anything other than go along with it.

Brian also told concerned people that he planned to start an orphanage for kids. His motives for everything appeared altruistic, and his plans seemed at least possible. He would tell this to anybody who would listen and they would congratulate him on his bravery and sacrifice for the orphans in South America. They would tell me how lucky I was to have such a selfless committed husband who cared so much about others.

I hoped they were right. I told myself repeatedly that it really would be fun and educational, and we would come back to the States with great tales of our adventures. However, no matter how hard I tried to convince myself of this, my instincts worked overtime warning me otherwise. I was too afraid of Brian to do anything about it though, and didn't want to risk him taking the children without me. The ability to think independently and stand up for what I believed in was lost by now. We were two people in the flesh, but in every other way we were one person. We were Brian. He dominated and controlled the thinking, feeling, and decision-making. I had gradually lost my personal identity and soul to him and didn't even realize it.

After a month of wandering aimlessly around Chile, we ended up penniless and homeless on a beach. Brian may have been able to get away with his charm and impulsive choices in the U.S., but the Chileans weren't buying it. Doors shut everywhere he turned. I felt exhausted, afraid, betrayed, hopeless, confused and angry. This appeared to be a potentially tragic experience. Brian even gave up hope and told me to get used to being homeless - I would learn to like it!

Becoming homeless in a foreign country with three small children jarred me out of my spiritual and psychological lethargy. I had no choice but to see the reality of my life and the truth of what kind of man my husband really was. My tightly held illusion of us being a relatively normal, happy, good Christian family popped like a bubble that night on the beach.

I had reached a crossroads, intuitively knowing that the choices I made in the next few hours and days would define the rest of our lives. I was not prepared for this in any way: mentally, financially, spiritually, emotionally…Why do crossroads happen when one is least ready for it?

When morning finally came, I went for a walk on the beach as the sun gently warmed the chilly damp air. Stepping around sleeping bodies, I thought about how my life was turning out, and how my daughters were being affected. It was not what I wanted for us. But there was no denying, as I took a ruthless look at my life, that the only reason for it was because I had made my own unwise choices. No one had ever held a gun to my head and made me do anything. Sure, I had my share of unfair life circumstances. Up until that morning, it had made sense to blame all sorts of things and people in life for my unhappiness. But that morning on the beach, I admitted that I was at least partially responsible for being there.

The great thing about accepting responsibility, I discovered, was that it gave me the power to change my life if I didn't like it! I decided to take ownership of my life and choices. What was done was done up to that point. I couldn't change the past, but it didn't mean I had to accept it as my future. It was the most freeing and empowering awakening I had ever experienced. As I took ownership of my life and choices, I realized that I would have to stand up to Brian and stop submissively doing and thinking whatever he demanded.

I knew the girls and I needed divine assistance and I expected Brian to fight me on my new independence. After all, I was supposed to be submissive and follow him, even if he demanded we live homeless. However, in spite of that deeply ingrained and faulty religious mindset, I sensed that God was somehow going to help me. I knew I was doing the right thing to try to protect my girls.

Before going back to our little shelter, I tearfully prayed one of the most heartfelt prayers I have ever prayed: "Help us God!" My inner pain and fear were so overwhelming that I couldn't choke out much more. But I knew that God heard and understood the unspoken words in it. I also resolved to put God back on the throne of my heart. I realized that Brian had subtly usurped that place that should only belong to God. I didn't understand the dynamics and meaning of everything yet, but I knew two things for sure that morning: One, God needed to be first place in my heart; and two, I needed to protect my children.

Gathering all the courage I could muster, I went back to Brian. I calmly told him with a firm resolution that secretly surprised me: "I'm getting us back home." Brian shocked me by silently nodding his head, allowing me to take the lead. That scared me worse than if he had argued with me! I was terrified to take on this new role of an assertive woman, and angry that I had to learn how to do it here of all places and times. I had no idea how to get us out of the mess we were in when we literally had not a cent left and had alienated our friends and family. Even the local churches and missions had rejected us. The task before me seemed impossible.

God honored my choice to put him back into first place in my life and to protect my daughters. He directed my steps that day, miraculously brought provision, and in a couple of weeks we were all safely back home in the States without having spent another night outside.

I thought that life couldn't get any worse than what I had experienced on that trip, but was wrong. I just wanted to go home, forget about that nightmare, and resume the decent life I had known before. However, after we arrived back in the States, the following year became a worse nightmare as my husband spiraled into a cruel and dangerous dark hole that threatened again to destroy us all. I wondered often if this hole had a bottom to it.

There is a common belief that adversity makes a person stronger. Brian proved this is a myth. The *right response* to adversity makes a person stronger. Brian's response to the disaster in South America was to discard any semblance of goodness. He chose anger, bitterness and blaming, and engaged in foolish and dangerous behavior that hurt anyone who was unfortunate to be in his path.

As I mentioned at the beginning, I eventually made a strategic plan of escape, and quietly, with the support of a few others, followed through. I did not have my life mapped out, and the following year as a newly single mom without financial support from my furious husband was very difficult. Sometimes life was so hard and discouraging I thought I had made a mistake and it would be better to go back just to have some provision and stability. But through the grace of God, we made it without that happening.

Today, I am free of toxic relationships and my children are thriving. I firmly believe our newly found happiness and hope is all due to a loving God who must have cheered to see me finally leave the abuse. I had plenty of obstacles to face though:

- The country was in a recession, government resources were dwindling, my husband was dangerously angry and refused to financially contribute to us, and years of being without a job hindered my being able to reenter the workforce.

- I was terribly confused about love. I scorned the one man who offered me true love and respect, while being drawn back into the cycle of toxic relationships with "exciting" men who wanted to "protect" me.

- I needed to rebuild strained relationships that my husband had nearly destroyed.

- I had to help my children and myself heal and recover in the midst of the crushing stress of trying to start life anew.

God's grace, forgiveness and love not only allowed us to change course, but to do it with his blessing and help. We experienced the truth of Romans 8:28, "We know that all things work together for good for those who love God, who are called according to his purpose." In hindsight, the painful crossroads of my life were the greatest opportunities. They were an invitation to a life of peace and happiness.

You may be at your own crossroads. Life may seem completely hopeless, confusing and unfair. Fear and uncertainty may color every moment. GOD LOVES YOU. He wants you to feel safe, loved, treasured and honored.

Remember what I said about having hot chocolate with him? He wants this close fellowship with you also. You may do something other than talk over hot chocolate, but whatever it is, take the time to be with him. As you draw near to him, having faith that he loves, accepts and approves of you, you will get the strength and help you need. James 4:8 promises, "Draw near to God, and he will draw near to you…" and Isaiah 41:10, "Do not fear, for I am with you, do not be afraid, for I am your God; I will strengthen you, I will help you, I will uphold you with my victorious right hand."

God deeply cherishes you, his daughter. Take Zephaniah 3:17 to heart. Hear your heavenly Father whispering to you right now, *Daughter,*

I am in your midst, a Warrior who saves. I rejoice over you with joy; you will be quiet in my love.

Chapter One

Defining the Difference between Abusive and Challenging

1. The Abuser Defined
2. But He's Mostly Good!
3. Isolation Is Dangerous
4. Where Is Your Marriage on This Scale?
5. Is His Fruit Good or Toxic?
6. Toxic and a Fool
7. He Says, "Judge Not!"
8. Be Cautious of Testimonies
9. A Final Question

1. The Abuser Defined

Was my husband just a jerk, or was there a more serious character flaw? I asked myself this often. It was hard to decipher, especially since our relationship started out exciting and fun, and we enjoyed many good times together. As the years went by, Brian's behavior became increasingly hurtful. My emotional health seemed to hang on by the thinnest of threads. I wondered, am I losing my sanity or am I truly in a dysfunctional and perhaps dangerous relationship?

Dr. Jeanne King, author of *All But My Soul: Abuse Beyond Control*, explains the difference well:

> I think being abusive is a rather general way of describing behavior that violates you as a person; your rights, your space, your choices, yourself. It can come out of frustration, stress, lowered inhibitions, insecurity, fear, vulnerability, or any combination of the above.

> Being an abuser, on the other hand in the classical sense, refers to a person that fulfills a specific criteria. And when engaged in an intimate relationship with this person, a specific criteria of defining characteristics exist which are "intimate partner violence."
>
> The criteria for intimate partner violence consists of: possessiveness, controlling behavior, lack of empathy, externalization of blame, isolation of victimized partner, and the use of battering to create and maintain a relationship of unequal power. (1)

That is the primary difference between those who are challenging to be with in a relationship because they don't know better, and those who are truly abusive. There can be many things that cause people to behave in hurtful ways such as drug use, stress, financial pressure and illness. Many people have not learned how to treat others with integrity and decency because it hasn't been modeled for them. They act thoughtlessly because that's what they know.

However, they are not trying to have power and control over others because they think they are entitled to it. They just don't understand how to speak and act in a way that is beneficial and respectful. Counseling, education, mentoring and accountability can often change this for a happier future.

Abuse, however, is a mentality of entitlement. Abusers do not generally respond well to counseling and education because they do not see themselves as part of any problem. Abusers have a goal, and that is power and control over others regardless of what it takes to obtain it. Abusers are not hampered by a healthy conscience like the rest of us are. They steal a victim's identity. Some, like me, see it as a form of murder.

As I said earlier, I had lost my identity to Brian. It happened so subtly that I didn't even recognize the process. Brian did all of our thinking and decision-making. When our relationship first started, I saw this as being strong, protective and decisive. It was romantic and flattering. As time went by, I occasionally asserted my independent opinion about something only to be punished. I learned it was better to just accept what he demanded for the sake of peace. Physically we were two people, but in every other way we were one person - we were Brian.

It was at my crossroads in Chile, that I became aware of how much control he had taken of me. I realized I no longer knew myself as a distinct individual. I literally had a feeling that somewhere along the line I had died, without knowing precisely when it had happened. Realizing this was a significant part of my awakening into the person I am today.

Think abuse is limited to physical violence? It's not. Brian never laid a hand on me violently, but he controlled and terrorized me nonetheless. He used tactics of verbal, emotional, financial, social, sexual, psychological and spiritual abuse to keep me in line with what he wanted.

The THREAT of physical violence was there. I remember him preparing and serving me dinner one day. While we ate, he "joked" about knowing how to kill with a local herb placed in food, and it appearing like a natural heart attack to a coroner. He "joked" about slicing pets throats when he tired of them. He attempted to poison neighbor's pets.

If he felt a neighbor or business associate had crossed him, he planned their "accidental" death. He would even demand I pass along his threats of murder to men he believed had flirted with me. So no, he never had to punch me in the face. I was scared enough knowing what he was capable of. I didn't do anything that might arouse violent anger toward the kids or myself.

Lundy Bancroft, author of *Why Does He Do That? Inside the Minds of Angry and Controlling Men*, offers this if you are still wondering about the violence issue:

> Has he ever trapped you in a room and not let you out?
>
> Has he ever raised a fist as if he were going to hit you?
>
> Has he ever thrown an object that hit you or nearly did?
>
> Has he ever held you down or grabbed you to restrain you?
>
> Has he ever shoved, poked, or grabbed you?
>
> Has he ever threatened to hurt you?
>
> If the answer to any of these questions is yes, then we can stop wondering whether he'll ever be violent; he already has been.(2)

Understanding the difference between an abuser, and someone who just needs some guidance through a difficult situation, is important to making knowledgeable choices about your relationship. We don't want to label (albeit challenging) people as abusers without there being a pattern of abusive behavior. Nevertheless, if the signs of abuse are there, then it is better to accept that and move forward with that knowledge. Ignorance will only cause unproductive choices, passivity and more pain. In many cases, it ends in tragedy.

As hard as it may be to consider that your husband may be an abuser, it will still help you and maybe him eventually. As wisely said in John 8:32, "and you will know the truth, and the truth will make you free." So let's be open to the truth about your spouse and your relationship. Then you will be well on your way to getting the answers and help you need.

If you have not, it would be worth your time to read the interview of Lundy Bancroft at *Pandora's Project*. Louise, the interviewer, asked him a great question about recognizing the signs of abuse:

> Louise: Some of our members are really hard on themselves because they didn't recognize the signs of an abuser. Yet you've written that there is no one stereotype of an abuser - could you elaborate on that?
>
> Lundy: Abusers don't usually show themselves early in a relationship — they can look pretty much like other men as dating is beginning. There are things you can watch for, but they aren't usually things anyone warned you about, so it's not your fault that you didn't know they were danger signs. Here are a few of them:
>
> 1) Jealousy and possessiveness — which can be flattering, but are actually really bad news
>
> 2) Being controlling
>
> 3) Always making everything your fault
>
> 4) He seems to be on really bad terms with his former partners
>
> 5) He seems to have bad attitudes toward women in general
>
> 6) He gets really disrespectful at times, then makes excuses for it
>
> 7) He does things you asked him not to do, perhaps too many favors for example, and it's hard to back him off

8) He pressures you regarding sex, such as wanting sex sooner in the relationship than you do

9) He's self-focused, and doesn't show that much interest in your tastes or opinions

10) He gets intimidating when he's angry, and then blames that on you.

There are various others, but these are critical ones to begin with.(3)

I want to emphasize that abusers don't usually show up holding a sign announcing their intentions. Even though I had been professionally trained as a domestic violence advocate, I still completely missed the signs with Brian, or justified them. So please don't beat yourself up over it. Be forgiving and kind to yourself, and focus on what you can do now to change your future.

2. But He's Mostly Good!

Some behavior I considered "mostly good" when actually it was abusive and controlling. As a positive person who easily forgives, I had no problem focusing on the good things about Brian. I think though, that after a while I focused on them more out of a need to mentally survive than truly believing in his goodness. No one is completely good or bad. Family and neighbors often remember the worst criminals in history with fondness. Even with my professional training, I ignored far too many signs. I can see that now but could not, or would not, face it back then.

For example, one lie of Brian's I believed was his explanation for his mysterious disappearances. Brian would disappear in the middle of the night without a word to me that he was leaving, where he was going, or how long he would be gone. I had no idea what to tell questioning people or our children. It was bewildering and heart breaking to experience as things began to spiral more out of control.

I hated his disappearances, and worried endlessly, wondering what was happening and why he would do this to us. When he would finally come home, he would say something to this effect: *Honey, I just needed to get away to study my Bible and pray. You know that when there is a special calling on someone's life, like there is on mine, that we have to obey God and hide ourselves away with him when he calls. You have to accept that when God calls me away to be alone with him, that I have to go. I shouldn't have to explain that to you.*

The concept of courtesy escaped him. I'm embarrassed now to say I actually thought that, though rude, he really was going off to pray. In hindsight, I realize that I was naive of the signs of drug use/binges. I also chose to ignore my gut instincts telling me what my mind couldn't comprehend. My being naive didn't make his behavior good. It was a lie and very hurtful to the children and myself.

Another thing he would tell me sometimes was that he was discipling a new employee at work. This required staying at work late, sometimes even overnight. Brian would share stories of the employee's progress and growth as a Christian under his wise guidance. As I write this, I shake my head with disgust that I actually believed these stories. Although, who wouldn't be supportive of helping someone who is troubled and needs encouragement? I certainly supported it. I really wanted to believe it. What a good man Brian was to so willingly and sacrificially help others! I would come to realize much later that the only "discipling" Brian was doing was drugging and partying with his new buddy.

Jealousy was another trap for me. In the beginning, Brian made his jealousy appear so masculine, noble and loving. But it never was good and never was love. Jealousy is abuse plain and simple, and fatal for many.

My intuition usually knew something was amiss, but until my mind could understand, I didn't know what else to do but accept the explanation offered. In hindsight, I wish I had trusted my intuition and talked to someone who might have had insight into why I was feeling so bad about things so noble. So consider that what you think might be mostly good, might really be abusive. They might really be warning flags of upcoming trouble. Talking to an objective third party, like an advocate at a women's shelter, can open your eyes to other possibilities.

Many people around us could see what Brian was doing and what a jerk he was. But Brian's conditioning and isolating had me believing that no one could be trusted. I actually believed him for a long time that we had a love so special and beautiful that inferior people would try to destroy it out of jealousy. The problem was, in Brian's world, everyone was inferior. I avoided people and was very defensive at the slightest suggestion Brian was less than perfect. People kept their concerns to themselves even though they saw plenty to worry about.

3. Isolation is Dangerous

Isolation is a hallmark of abuse. An abuser makes being separate from others seem so good, reasonable and even spiritual. If you are avoiding people, or are being kept from socializing with others - wake up! You are in an unhealthy relationship and it's not going to get better. A man who genuinely loves you and has nothing to hide will not "protect" you from family, friends and community. He may express concern over an issue with someone, but his intention will not be to tell you what you have to do. Rather, healthy couples talk about people and issues in a mutually respectful and supportive manner.

There is no justification for isolation. Isolation is what delusional and insecure people do to get and maintain power over others. This happens in cults and other unhealthy fringe groups. Jesus certainly doesn't promote this in any way. The Bible repeatedly encourages meeting with others for friendship, accountability, mentoring, growth and strength. Socializing is an important part of our growth. If your husband is telling you otherwise, he is telling you something that goes against the Bible.

Consider these biblical principles of sharing life with others:

Loving others as we love ourselves by demonstrating deliberate and purposeful respect, good will and benevolent concern for others. (Mark 12:26-31; John 13:34-35, 15:12; Romans 15:1-2)

Self-righteousness and arrogance are displayed when we treat others as inferior to us. God hates self-righteousness! (Romans 3:21-24; 1 John 1:8; Luke 18:9-14; Isaiah 5:21; Galatians 6:1-3)

Generosity toward others with our time and money. (1 John 3:17; 1 Timothy 6:17-19; Isaiah 58:10-11). Generosity is not just about writing out a check and walking away. God's generosity includes taking the time to talk with others, coming alongside them and helping them in their struggles.

We need each other to be healthy and strong. Being alone goes against God's principles of maturity in believers. Jesus modeled it for us. He wasn't an island to himself. He humbly and cheerfully socialized with men, women and children inside and outside the religious institution, showing great care and interest in them and their lives.

Brian believed that everyone was against us because we had something so special that they were jealous. If they weren't jealous then they were ignorant or hopelessly "religious." Or people were against us because we were the "chosen" of God and they weren't, and we had to live untainted lives apart from them. Does your husband display any of these attitudes?

The fact is, it is highly unlikely that everyone in your world is chomping at the bit to ruin your life and marriage. People aren't just sitting around wallowing in jealousy over your relationship, or trying to destroy your happiness to make themselves look good and feel better. Most people really are good, kind and want you to be happy. Most people want to get along and believe the best. However, the vast majority of people also have the objective freedom to see red flags in someone else's relationship. If people seem concerned about things, there is probably good reason for it!

On the flip side, I can think of numerous cases of church members and leaders turning a blind eye to abuse, or blaming the victim for it. This is very common in churches so please do not use them as the defining standard for what is or isn't appropriate behavior. You are more likely to get valuable feedback from people not attending your church, such as co-workers, support groups, helping agencies, friends and acquaintances.

Another red flag I ignored was isolation from his family. When we met, Brian claimed his family was corrupt and therefore it was necessary to protect me from them. He painted a picture of gross dysfunction, lying, and unfairness that made me feel sorry for him and never want to be around them. I couldn't believe how evil they were and why they would ever want to hurt him and our relationship. Brian was blessed to have gotten away from such terrible people!

I should have recognized that as the red flag of an abuser that it was. But, Brian always had compelling reasons for everything. It wasn't until the end of our marriage that I realized they had been lies designed to keep me protected from the truth his family and friends would have warned me of. Interestingly, I found out after I left him that he had also told them terrible lies about me to keep them from wanting to talk to me. Understandably, his family was distant and distrustful of me, even though I had never remotely been involved in any of the things

Brian had claimed about me. By lying to all of us, he effectively isolated me and protected himself from exposure.

See how smooth abusers are? They must keep the truth suppressed! That is done by controlling information and manipulating people and events so that they are not exposed. Up until the end I couldn't grasp that Brian's testimony could be false. It was the hardest thing for me to comprehend - someone faking a testimony! I'll talk about this more in a bit. It was after I found out the lies he had told about me to his family that I realized I had been fooled, along with them. It worked for quite a while, but God caused the truth to eventually surface. Brian was smooth and smart - and a complete fraud. But all I saw was what he wanted me to see: a strong and gifted man of God taking care of his family.

4. Where Is Your Marriage on This Scale?

Let's look at where your marriage may be on a scale of HEALTHY to STRUGGLING to dangerously TOXIC:

<u>A Healthy Marriage</u>

There is no such thing as a 'perfect marriage.' However, a couple in a healthy marriage enjoys a substantially good partnership. Some characteristics of a healthy marriage are:

- You both feel happy and safe, alone and together.
- You are able to communicate in an open and honest way with each other.
- You can laugh and de-escalate conflicts when they arise.
- You share mutual and separate friends.
- You have a vision of the future and work together as a team to get there.
- You both take responsibility for the good and the bad.
- You both forgive and can say, "I'm sorry."
- Neither habitually engages in negative attitudes of criticism, contempt, defensiveness or stonewalling.
- You accept each other the way you are with no demand to change.
- You motivate each other to pursue dreams and live life to the fullest.
- You help each other with chores.

<u>A Struggling Marriage</u>

As we move into the middle, we have marriages that struggle at times. Most marriages do and there is always room for growth. *These relationships are characterized more by what is absent rather than what is abusive.* Ignorance and immaturity are usually the cause of a struggle. Knowledge, and with time maturity, make things right. A couple can work through these problems by prayerfully studying God's Word and getting competent counseling as appropriate. Sometimes there is an underlying health issue that needs addressed, or financial and communication issues that can be resolved with professional guidance. There is usually a solution for the source of the struggle, and both marriage partners want to find out what it is and resolve the problem.

If you fall into this middle category, please do not use this book as a way to rationalize giving up on your marriage. Prayerfully examine your motives. Although you may be unhappy in your current relationship, it is better to stay and work through the problems. It can be completely turned around if you are both willing!

A Toxic Marriage

Marriages that fall into this extreme are the focus of this book. Your spouse, through the intentional use of pain and intimidation to control you, has breached the marriage covenant dangerously and destructively. It is for Christian women who find themselves trapped in fear and false theology that I strive to bring forth the light of God's truth to dispel the darkness.

Characteristics of a toxic marriage are:

- You feel afraid of and anxious to please your husband.
- You go along with whatever he says and does.
- You check in often with him to report where you are and what you are doing.
- He monitors you.
- He has a temper and is jealous and possessive.
- He has been physically violent toward you, children or pets.
- He sabotages your job, school or social occasions.
- You are restricted from seeing family and friends.
- You rarely go out in public without your husband.
- You have limited access to money, credit cards, or the car.
- You are experiencing personality changes, such as going from outgoing to withdrawn.

- You feel depressed, anxious, drained, scared, ashamed, confused or suicidal.
- He uses dominance, humiliation, isolation, threats, intimidation, denial and blame to manipulate you.
- You wonder if you are crazy and the one to blame for all the problems.
- He sexually forces or coerces you into things you don't want.

In spite of the drama and excitement surrounding Brian's supposed conversion and transformation, he was unable to hold to basic Christian tenants over the long haul. Matthew 7:15-21 says we can know the character of someone by their actions. Let's see if we can get more clarity by examining your husband's "fruit" in the light of God's Word.

5. Is His Fruit Good or Toxic?

Matthew 7:15-21, "(15) Beware of false prophets, who come to you in sheep's clothing but inwardly are ravenous wolves. (16) You will know them by their fruits. Are grapes gathered from thorns, or figs from thistles? (17) In the same way, every good tree bears good fruit, but the bad tree bears bad fruit. (18) A good tree cannot bear bad fruit, nor can a bad tree bear good fruit. (19) Every tree that does not bear good fruit is cut down and thrown into the fire. (20) Thus you will know them by their fruits. (21) Not everyone who says to me, 'Lord, Lord,' will enter the kingdom of heaven, but only the one who does the will of my Father in heaven."

According to Barnes notes on this passage:

> Verse 15:... A false prophet is a teacher of incorrect doctrine, or one falsely and unjustly laying claims to divine inspiration...Who come in sheep's clothing...The sheep is an emblem of innocence, sincerity, and harmlessness. To come in sheep's clothing is to assume the appearance of sanctity and innocence, when the heart is evil. Ravening wolves...they assumed the appearance of holiness in order that they might the more readily get the property of the people...

> Verse 16: Ye shall know them by their fruits - The Savior gives the proper test of their character. People do not judge of a tree by its leaves, or bark, or flowers, but by the fruit which it bears.

> The flowers may be beautiful and fragrant, the foliage thick and green; but these are merely ornamental. It is the "fruit" that is of chief service to man; and he forms his opinion of the nature and value of the tree by that fruit. So of pretensions to religion. The profession may be fair; but the "conduct" - the fruit - is to determine the nature of the principles.
>
> Verse 17: A corrupt tree - The word "corrupt" here does not signify, as our translation would seem to indicate, that the tree "had been" good, but had become "vitiated;" but that it was a tree of a useless character, of a nature that produced nothing beneficial.
>
> Verse 21: The Savior goes on to say that many, on the ground of a mere profession such as he had just referred to, would claim admittance into his kingdom. See Matthew 7:21; 1 Corinthians 1:26; 1 Corinthians 13:1-3… In this last place, Paul says that, though he spoke with the tongue of angels, and had the gift of prophecy, and could remove mountains, and had nor charity or love, all would be of no avail. (4)

Wow! Talk about an accurate description of many religious, yet abusive, husbands. Brian was certainly "a teacher of incorrect doctrine," "falsely and unjustly laying claims to divine inspiration" with "the appearance of sanctity and innocence, when the heart is evil," and "…assumed the appearance of holiness in order that they might the more readily get the property of the people." In this case, I would substitute "soul" for "property." Isn't that what abusers do? They steal our identity, our very soul from us.

In 2 Corinthians 13:5 Paul commanded, "Examine yourselves to see whether you are living in the faith. Test yourselves. Do you not realize that Jesus Christ is in you? Unless, indeed, you fail to meet the test!"

Jesus shows us what it means to "meet the test" of living in the faith in John 15:1-17,

> (1)I am the true vine, and my Father is the vine grower. (2) He removes every branch in me that bears no fruit. Every branch that bears fruit he prunes to make it bear more fruit. (3) You have already been cleansed by the word that I have spoken to you. (4) Abide in me as I abide in you. Just as the branch cannot bear fruit by itself unless it abides in the vine, neither can

you unless you abide in me. (5) I am the vine, you are the branches. Those who abide in me and I in them bear much fruit, because apart from me you can do nothing. (6) Whoever does not abide in me is thrown away like a branch and withers; such branches are gathered, thrown into the fire, and burned. (7) If you abide in me, and my words abide in you, ask for whatever you wish, and it will be done for you. (8) My Father is glorified by this, that you bear much fruit and become my disciples. (9) As the Father has loved me, so I have loved you; abide in my love. (10) If you keep my commandments, you will abide in my love, just as I have kept my Father's commandments and abide in his love. (11) I have said these things to you so that my joy may be in you, and that your joy may be complete. (12) This is my commandment, that you love one another as I have loved you. (13) No one has greater love than this, to lay down one's life for one's friends. (14) You are my friends if you do what I command you. (15) I do not call you servants any longer, because the servant does not know what the master is doing; but I have called you friends, because I have made known to you everything that I have heard from my Father. (16) You did not choose me but I chose you. And I appointed you to go and bear fruit, fruit that will last, so that the Father will give you whatever you ask him in my name. (17) I am giving you these commands so that you may love one another.

What more does the Bible say about fruit? There are several kinds of fruit that will be evident in someone who is truly born again:

<ins>Fruit of Repentance</ins>

"Bear fruit worthy of repentance." (Matthew 3:8) Repentance means turning away from a self-ruled life to a God-ruled life. The Bible says that we are saved by faith alone, however there can be no faith in Christ without repentance and no repentance without faith: Ephesians 2:8-9, "(8) For by grace you have been saved through faith, and this is not your own doing; it is the gift of God, (9) not the result of works, so that no one may boast."

The fruit of repentance is seen when we realize we have offended the nature and character of our Lord and feel grief over it. We realize the majesty and holiness of God and hate anything that sets itself contrary to that. False repentance puts on a self-serving show when needed and doesn't produce lasting change. Genuine repentance (and the only kind the Lord receives) is grieved over anything that grieves the Lord, and the person genuinely CHANGES through the power of Christ in him/her.

Fruit of Good Works

"So that you may lead lives worthy of the Lord, fully pleasing to him, as you bear fruit in every good work and as you grow in the knowledge of God." (Colossians 1:10)

Titus 3:8 says, "I desire that you insist on these things, so that those who have come to believe in God may be careful to devote themselves to good works; these things are excellent and profitable to everyone."

I like what John Wesley said, "Do all the good you can, by all the means you can, in all the ways you can, in all the places you can, to all the people you can, as long as you ever can." Although good works do not get us to heaven, they do testify of our genuine faith. They are fruit that people can see and know that we are genuine.

Fruit of Thanksgiving

"Through him, then, let us continually offer a sacrifice of praise to God, that is, the fruit of lips that confess his name." (Hebrews 13:15)

"(6) As you therefore have received Christ Jesus the Lord, continue to live your lives in him, (7) rooted and built up in him and established in the faith, just as you were taught, abounding in thanksgiving." (Colossians 2:6-7)

Fruit of the Spirit

"(22) By contrast, the fruit of the Spirit is love, joy, peace, patience, kindness, generosity, faithfulness, (23) gentleness, and self-control. There is no law against such things. (24) And those who belong to Christ Jesus have crucified the flesh with its passions and desires. (25) If we live by the Spirit, let us also be guided by the Spirit." (Galatians 5:22-25)

All this fruit produces a harvest of righteousness: "Having produced the harvest of righteousness that comes through Jesus Christ for the glory and praise of God." (Philippians 1:11)

We know what good fruit looks like and what it produces. Let's look at fruit the Bible warns is toxic.

Toxic Fruit

"(19) Now the practices of the sinful nature are clearly evident: they are sexual immorality, impurity, sensuality (total irresponsibility, lack of self-control), (20) idolatry, sorcery, hostility, strife, jealousy, fits of anger, disputes, dissensions, factions [that promote heresies], (21) envy, drunkenness, riotous behavior, and other things like these. I warn you beforehand, just as I did previously, that those who practice such things will not inherit the kingdom of God." (Galatians 5:19-21 AMP)

To summarize Barnes notes on this passage, the works of the flesh are corrupt, un-renewed and made plain and well known. As you read this, can you see characteristics of abusers? Witchcraft is characterized by someone who attempts to impose their will on others, which is rebellion against God. Hatred is a lack of love that produces contention and strife. Strife here is tied to Romans 1:29 which is someone being filled with all unrighteousness, wickedness, greed, evil, full of envy, murder, strife, deceit, malice, gossips. Emulations is ardor or zeal in a bad cause, leading to strife. Wrath here is tied to 2 Corinthians 12:20 - strife, jealousy, angry tempers, disputes, slanders, gossip, arrogance, disturbances. Seditions is tied to Romans 16:17, "Now I urge you, brethren, keep your eye on those who cause dissensions and hindrances contrary to the teaching which you learned, and turn away from them."

To quote Barnes about those who will not inherit the kingdom of God:

> Shall not inherit the kingdom of God - Cannot possibly be saved; see the notes at 1 Corinthians 6:9-11. In regard to this passage, we may remark:...this passage is full of fearful admonition to those who indulge in any or all of these vices. Paul, inspired of God, has solemnly declared, that such cannot be saved. They cannot enter into the kingdom of heaven as they are. Nor is it desirable that they should. What would heaven be if filled up with adulterers, and fornicators, and idolaters, with the proud and envious, and with murderers, and drunkards? To call such a place heaven, would be an abuse of

the word. No one could wish to dwell there; and such people cannot enter into heaven...the human heart must be changed, or man cannot be saved. This follows of course. If such is its tendency, then there is a necessity for such a change as that in regeneration, in order that man may be happy and be saved... We should rejoice that such people cannot, with their present characters, be admitted to heaven...

How cheering the thought that there is one world where these vices are unknown; one world, all whose ample plains may be traversed, and the note of blasphemy shall never fall on the ear; one world, where virtue shall be safe from the arts of the seducer; one world where we may forever dwell, and not one reeling and staggering drunkard shall ever be seen; where there shall be not one family in want and tears from the vice of its unfaithful head! (emphasis mine)With what joy should we look forward to that world! With what ardor should we pant that it may be our own! (5)

These scriptures have identified unrepentant abusers, among others of ungodly character. If God will not allow them in his home, if he will not live with them, then why would we ever assume that he demands it of us? God does not have a double standard, and his opinion of those who deliberately cause pain to others is evident - he's not turning a blind eye to it and he's not afraid to call it what it is! We don't have to be afraid either. In fact when we call sin and hypocrisy what it is, we come into agreement with him - a good and safe place to be. "What then shall we say to all these things? If God is for us, who can be [successful] against us?" (Romans 8:31 AMP)

6. Toxic and a Fool

Another way to look at this is to read what the Bible says about fools and foolishness. One can easily replace the word "fool" with the word "abuser." The description is the same for both. An abusive husband truly is a fool and his fruit is toxic! Here are some characteristics of fools found in the book of Proverbs:

- Fools don't learn from their mistakes but keep repeating them (26:11)

- They despise knowledge (1:22)

- Are quick-tempered (12:16)
- Deceitful (14:8)
- They don't want to understand, but rather to air their own opinions (18:2-3)
- They despise wisdom and discipline (1:5-7)
- They lie and manipulate (10:18-19)
- Doing wrong is fun for them (10:23-25)
- They will not make things right with others when they have hurt someone (14:8-10)
- They trust in themselves (28:26)
- They are hot-heads (29:11)
- They spend unwisely (21:20)
- They bring grief and bitterness to their family (17:25)
- They despise those who are wise (23:9)
- They are reckless and careless (14:16)

So what kind of fruit is your husband producing? Fruit of wisdom or fruit of foolishness? Fruit of righteousness or works of the flesh? If he is genuinely a Christian as he may claim, then he will be growing, as we all should, in grace and love. It doesn't mean he won't make mistakes. We all do. But he will accept correction and instruction in living a biblical Christian life. Good character and integrity should dominate the flaws.

Religion produces some truly passionate though dangerously deluded people. If his actions don't line up with the Bible, then stop being manipulated with the title. Accept that it is bogus. Don't feel guilty for seeing and accepting the truth rather than the lies. When I no longer bought the line of "Christian" nonsense Brian fed me, he gave up on it.

7. He Says "Judge Not!"

Have you ever had Matthew 7:1 thrown in your face whenever you questioned someone's beliefs or behavior? ("Do not judge, so that you may not be judged.") Pastor David Curtis at The Berean Bible Church has an excellent teaching that clarifies the real meaning of it:

> Many people have misunderstood Jesus' admonition concerning judging. When Jesus says that we are not to judge, many people have interpreted that to mean that we are not to engage in any form of analysis or evaluation of others. In other words, this line of thinking says that we cannot conclude that a person's behavior or lifestyle is wrong, and that they are consequently wrong for engaging in it. Those who would like to justify all manner of evil use this verse to chasten anyone who would take a stand for righteousness.
>
> This verse is also misused when referring to other people's religious beliefs. Some people seem to say that we must sacrifice our ability to discriminate in decision making. Such a position would require that we exercise no discernment. There is a sense in which we are not to judge people, but we will see in this study that there is a sense in which we, as believers, are required to judge others. (6)

There are numerous verses that command us to judge righteous judgment. Matthew 7:15-16 commands us to evaluate who is a true and false prophet. 1 John 4:1-2 tells us to test the spirits to see if they are of God. 1 Corinthians 10:15 says to judge what is being said, as in to weigh carefully and form an opinion or consideration. 2 Thessalonians 3:6 commands us to withdraw from brethren who walk disorderly. This requires making a judgment call. Romans 16:17 tells us to avoid brethren who cause division and offense. 1 Corinthians 5:6-7 says to purge out the "old leaven." There are several more verses, but these show that obviously we have to use some sort of judgment with others.

Pastor David also shares three attitudes that comprise righteous judgment:

> First, we are not to have a self-righteous judgmental attitude. Philippians 2:3 says "Do nothing from selfish ambition or conceit, but in humility regard others as better than yourselves."
>
> Secondly, we are not to judge the motives of others. We should not attempt to become the judge of another person's thoughts, the motives of their heart, or attempt to enter into the court of their conscience. Jeremiah 17:10 says "I the Lord test the mind and search the heart, to give to all according to their ways, according to the fruit of their doings."

Thirdly, we are not to judge hypocritically. The one who is quick to detect the minor faults of others while blind to, or unconcerned about, their own serious sins is a hypocrite. Matthew 7:3-5 says, "Why do you see the speck in your neighbor's eye, but do not notice the log in your own eye? 4 Or how can you say to your neighbor, 'Let me take the speck out of your eye,' while the log is in your own eye? 5 You hypocrite, first take the log out of your own eye, and then you will see clearly to take the speck out of your neighbor's eye." A "hypocrite" is the actor of a part, one pretending to be very zealous as to the requirements of holiness, while himself living in neglect and great sin...be faithful in dealing with yourself, unsparingly judging yourself before God, putting away out of your heart and life whatsoever you know to be displeasing unto God. (6)

I hope that this helps to relieve you of any guilt you have been carrying over seeing and questioning things that you suspect are not right. God wants you to do that! God has given his children discernment to make us aware and protect us from those who would cause us harm. Keep your heart clear with God and thank him every time he helps you to see through pretension and deception. On that note, use your discernment when you hear testimonies...

8. Be Cautious of Testimonies

I didn't find out the biblical truth about headship and submission until after I left Brian. Had I understood it earlier, I would have gotten the girls and myself out quicker. In the meantime, as I struggled to hold things together, I leaned on the certainty that Brian's testimony was real and his abusiveness was just a passing phase. I hoped that he really was a good guy who just needed time to work through some things and then everything would be okay.

I grew up reading books and hearing on television or at church countless testimonials about bad people turned good after accepting Christ into their hearts. Drug addicts and alcoholics instantly delivered from addictions. Criminals walking away from a life of crime. Broken relationships restored. Sexual trauma healed. The list is long, and I am NOT saying God doesn't save, heal and deliver. He absolutely does! I am saying that there are fraudulent testimonies used to manipulate people, and your husband's might be one of them.

Brian's testimony was one of the most dramatic I had heard. He claimed that in prison God brought him instant deliverance from a long life of hard-core drug abuse and dealing, prostitution, violence, gangs, and other serious criminal behavior. When I met him, his testimony seemed genuine and glorifying to God. Instant deliverance from deplorable lifelong behavior that had begun as a young boy? Sure! God can do anything! Brian even claimed a miraculous healing from an STD, verified by the prison doctor.

Brian seemed thrilled to have been set free from his former life, learned the Bible inside out while in prison, preached when he could, and believed God had called him to be a preacher to the world. Everything was so spiritual and appeared completely valid. I guess I wouldn't have known what invalid looked like though since I didn't even consider testimonies could be false.

I was naïve and trusting - one of the main reasons abusers, con artists and predators target Christians. My marriage to Brian was a rude awakening to the existence of phony testimonies. Brian kept this facade of devout Christianity for the first three years of our marriage. When he gave it up, I still clung to it. Except for isolated incidents when he needed some extra advantage to manipulate me into something, Brian stopped pretending to be a Christian. He went back to drinking and drugging, and was furious with God for not making him a preacher.

Brian's actions, words and reasoning were so conflicting, that I always felt off balance and like I was going a little crazy. Add to it that "Paul" stayed in the mix, and I retreated within myself almost completely. I stayed focused on my daughters and tried to not go crazy with Brian's world. At least he continued to work, provide and was not physically violent, so I figured everything would eventually work out. It didn't.

I now have a healthy caution toward people who claim to be radically saved and changed overnight. Again, I am NOT saying God doesn't deliver in amazing ways. But it is foolish to accept every testimony offered at face value. Christianity is a favorite escape for people who need to hide and want to prey on trusting and generous people. I have found in the years since, that while God does perform miracles, a person's core character is not normally changed overnight. Instantaneous change of character is rare. While a drug addict may be miraculously delivered from his addiction at a prayer meeting, it takes time for his ingrained way of thinking to become renewed.

If what he claims is just for show, he can pretend for a long time if he has strong enough willpower. However, the truth will eventually come out. TIME and FRUIT are the precious qualifiers of what is genuine and what is false. In the years that I have personally helped victims of domestic abuse and violence, it is sickening how often the abuser claims to be a Christian, is a pastor or other church leader, or otherwise active in church.

I held on to Brian's original testimony for dear life, thinking the setback was temporary and he just needed me to pray him through a rough time. I was so blind. He knew it too. He took full advantage of my trust, naivety, and spiritual faith. My plea to you is to not disregard bad behavior because he has given you a spiritual testimony. ANYONE can do that.

Pastor Jeff Crippen compares a man with a false testimony to a fool in Proverbs in his message *You Cannot Drive Abuse Out of the Abuser*:

> "Crush a fool in a mortar with a pestle along with crushed grain, yet his folly will not depart from him." (Proverbs 27:22) The fool in Proverbs is not merely some simple-minded person. Nope. This fool is a wicked individual. You can check this out for yourself if you want by simply reading the occurrences of "fool" in this book of Holy Scripture. And many of the descriptions of this fool given us by Solomon describe the abuser we know so well perfectly.
>
> So, look at this verse cited above. What does it tell us about the fool/abuser? It says that you can sooner grind him up in a flour-making machine (a mortar and pestle in those days) and get his blood out than you can use even the most severe methods on him to "bleed him" dry of his abuse. Which is all to say this: you can't fix an abuser… Not this guy who so often claims to be a Christian, but whose very essence of personhood is a profound sense of entitlement to power and control and who feels quite justified in using whatever evil tactics he needs to employ to get what he wants. You can't fix him. That is what these divinely inspired and inerrant words are telling us.

To many people, this fact seems disturbing. I mean, can't Christ change anyone? Aren't we as Christians supposed to "have faith" in the Lord's ability to give anyone a new heart and do whatever we can to lead such people to salvation in Christ? Christ gives a new heart to anyone who calls upon Him in real faith and repentance. But abusers don't do so. For all their common claims that they have changed, that they have really repented, for all the crocodile tears they shed, they do not humbly come to Christ in genuine faith, exercising real repentance. Crush them, winnow them, sift them all you like, their folly is not going to depart from them.

This seems disturbing to many people, but I find it a source of the very beginning of freedom from abuse. When an abuse victim comes to clearly understand that not only is her abuser an abuser, but that there is nothing she can do to change him by driving his abusive mentality out of him, then she can begin to take steps to get free. (7)

9. A Final Question

My final question to you is this: How does your husband's behavior make you feel?

Does it make you feel loved, cared about, secure, and happy? Or does it make you feel anxious, worthless, crazy, or depressed? Your feelings are a major indicator that his behavior is either toxic or not. That applies to anyone in your life. You don't have to understand why to intuitively know the truth. Pay attention to how his behavior makes you feel. If you are feeling bad, then something is probably wrong with it and warrants further investigation.

Honor your gut instincts. If you have been shutting them down, start by acknowledging them to God when they come up: "Lord, I am feeling _____ right now. Something isn't right. Thank you for protecting my children and me, and for helping me to see truth. As truth is revealed, give me the wisdom and strength to know how to respond to it."

I trust that by now you have determined if you are indeed in a toxic, abusive relationship. Hopefully Scripture has cleared up any confusion you had about the genuineness of your husband's claim of faith in God and Christian tenants. In the next chapter, we will lay the foundation for accurately interpreting what Scripture says about his headship and your submission.

Chapter Two
How to Rightly Interpret Scripture

1. Conflict between My Heart and My Head
2. Why You Should Read the Bible for Yourself
3. Six Principles for Discernment

1. Conflict between My Heart and My Head

As a devoted Christian wife and mother in an abusive marriage, I suffered with guilt, confusion and fear as I tried everything in my power to save our marriage. I attempted to do this under a religious belief system that undermined my desire to be happy and raise my children in an emotionally healthy environment.

I felt in my heart that demanding absolute submission of me with no way out was wrong. It just did not agree with the character of the God whom I deeply loved and followed. However, my religious beliefs were so deeply ingrained that I couldn't wrap my mind around anything different.

I desperately wanted to see the truth in the Bible, plain and simple. I wanted to ease the guilt that plagued me for not just accepting that the abuse wasn't worse. Try harder… Pray more… Be more submissive… Be more understanding… Be more enthusiastic in the bedroom… I hated it!

As I had been taught by traditional theology, physical adultery, abandonment or death was the only way out of a marriage. Since Brian was very much alive and wasn't leaving me, and I couldn't verify an affair, it appeared I was condemned to live with the abuse if I wanted to stay in God's favor.

However, God answers every heart's cry for truth! It has taken time for me to be able to receive the glorious truth about what God (not man) says about headship and submission. It really is very simple and full of hope for you! I eagerly share it, trusting that his simple yet powerful truths will set you free as they did me.

In Isaiah 1:18, God is heartbroken over his people's rebellion and corruption and he calls out to them: "Come now, let us argue it out..." (to prove, decide, judge, rebuke, reprove, correct, and be right). Ephesians 5:17 admonishes us to firmly understand God's will: "So do not be foolish, but understand what the will of the Lord is."

It may be hard to accept that what you believe about your relationship and God may be wrong. God wants us to examine and question things. He never asks us to take what anyone says about him at face value and structure our lives around it. We are thinking and reasoning beings in a world full of fallacy and error. We please God when we take things to him and examine the veracity of it.

When my eyes were finally opened to the fact that many of my beliefs were wrong and the source of unnecessary heartache, I was relieved to discover the truth. It took time for it to make sense though, and for my mind to be renewed. Satan does not want you to know the truth, because it will set you and your children free from bondage and destruction.

God wants you to know what is true and right so that you can make good choices and live in the light and freedom of his love and care. He has set forth some healthy guidelines for us to follow, and to help us know what to do about the difficult situations we find ourselves in. There is an answer and hope!

Let's keep in mind some principles in the Bible as we question what we have been taught about headship and submission. The Bible is either going to reinforce what we think, or reprove and correct thinking that is in error. My goal is not to tell you what to do, but to arm you with knowledge so you can make the best decisions for yourself and your family. There are six principles to keep in mind as we explore God's Word.

2. Why You Should Read the Bible for Yourself

<u>It is life!</u>

"It is the spirit that gives life; the flesh is useless. The words that I have spoken to you are spirit and life." (John 6:63) "But first and most importantly seek (aim at, strive after) His kingdom and His righteousness [His way of doing and being right—the attitude and character of

God], and all these things will be given to you also." (Matthew 6:33 AMP)

Jesus is saying that if we put him first, everything else will eventually come into proper place and priority in our lives. God's kingdom is the rule and reign of Jesus Christ in the personal lives of those who are spiritually born again. His righteousness means we are in right-relationship with him, or we are giving top priority to cooperating with him.

"All these things will be given to you" reflects Philippians 4:19, "And my God will fully satisfy every need of yours according to his riches in glory in Christ Jesus." Now, our idea of what we need is probably different from God's! But God wants us to rest in his love and care for us, knowing that he will care for us perfectly in his wisdom and sovereignty. He is the giver of life!

It brings wisdom.

"(6) Do not forsake her, and she will keep you; love her, and she will guard you. (7) The beginning of wisdom is this: Get wisdom, and whatever else you get, get insight. (8) Prize her highly, and she will exalt you; she will honor you if you embrace her. (9) She will place on your head a fair garland; she will bestow on you a beautiful crown. (10) Hear, my child, and accept my words, that the years of your life may be many. (11) I have taught you the way of wisdom; I have led you in the paths of uprightness. (12) When you walk, your step will not be hampered; and if you run, you will not stumble." (Proverbs 4:6-12)

Who of us doesn't want wisdom? Especially when we are in a toxic relationship and don't know what to do. Jesus has the answer for every question we have! Seek for it and it will come. You may have several conflicting sources of information and advice coming at you, causing uncertainty and fear. The best thing I did was to take all these things to God and confess I didn't have a clue what to do, and worse of all, I was too scared to do anything, but too scared not to do anything!

I can't say that God ever wrote on the wall telling me precisely what he wanted me to do. However, in hindsight, I can see that he was leading me. He was giving me wisdom. He was guiding my choices. Much of it I had to do in faith, not really ever knowing if I was doing the right thing or not.

God honored my asking him for wisdom and direction. My faith that he was answering that prayer pleased him. In the end, everything worked out. I did make some mistakes along the way, but when I realized it, I immediately went back to the Lord and asked for help. He ALWAYS helped me through everything. Not once did he ever fail my daughters or me. Not once did he ever fail to fulfill his Word in my life. He will do the same for you too.

Speaking of mistakes, in hindsight, I also see that those were made when I was acting out of fear and haste. This leads to the next great reason for reading the Bible…

<u>It brings peace.</u>

"27 Peace I leave with you; My [perfect] peace I give to you; not as the world gives do I give to you. Do not let your heart be troubled, nor let it be afraid. [Let My perfect peace calm you in every circumstance and give you courage and strength for every challenge.]" (John 14:27 AMP)

"(6) Do not worry about anything, but in everything by prayer and supplication with thanksgiving let your requests be made known to God. (7) And the peace of God, which surpasses all understanding, will guard your hearts and your minds in Christ Jesus." (Philippians 4:6-7)

When we study the Bible, particularly the topic of peace, we receive great comfort and courage in the midst of conflict and turmoil. As I mentioned earlier, my mistakes were made when I took matters into my own hands out of fear and being in a hurry. As long as I abided in a peaceful state of mind and heart, somehow things would just work out. Urgent issues would often resolve themselves. When I became afraid and reacted, that's when things didn't go so well. I would encourage you to do a Bible study on peace. It will change your outlook and your life!

3. Six Principles for Discernment

<u>1. God is the ultimate source of authority.</u>

Timothy 3:16-17 says "(16) All scripture is inspired by God and is useful for teaching, for reproof, for correction, and for training in

righteousness, (17) so that everyone who belongs to God may be proficient, equipped for every good work."

"God is the ultimate authority simply because He is "the LORD, and there is no other." (Isaiah 45:18)

"(16) For by Him all things were created in heaven and on earth, [things] visible and invisible, whether thrones or dominions or rulers or authorities; all things were created and exist through Him [that is, by His activity] and for Him. (17) And He Himself existed and is before all things, and in Him all things hold together. [His is the controlling, cohesive force of the universe.]" (Colossians 1:16-17 AMP)

When there is a conflict between a person's belief and God's Word, then we must side with God. Today's culture is producing many unbiblical or extra-biblical teachings and practices. Whatever error it is, it is a result of incorrectly interpreting the Bible. You may feel it is confusing to know the difference, but really it isn't if you understand the principles of correctly interpreting the Bible. God wants us to understand. Satan is the author of confusion, not God.

God knows your past, your future, and he knows your heart and that of everyone around you. You can be completely open and honest with him about your questions, your fears, your confusion, everything. He knows it anyway, and when you are willing to be transparent and imperfect before him, you honor him. Better to make mistakes in his presence rather than away from him! Make him the authority in your life now, exactly where you are, as you are. You will never regret it!

2. God will never reveal or speak something that contradicts what is written in the Bible.

Many modern day questionable "Christian" practices and teachings are justified by one Scripture, that God is doing "a new thing." (Isaiah 42:9) Has God turned his back on his Word and decided to do something completely new and out of character because he is bored with the old? Never! Do you see the modern day church and Christians accurately representing Jesus? Are we the spotless bride of Christ? Or do you see a sick, defiled and corrupt body ruled by apathy and compromise? Is God going to abandon us and raise up a new bride? No!

God is going to call us back to himself. He is going to deliver us from a shallow frivolous gospel that has led us astray. He is going to destroy every false gospel and put to shame every false teacher.

"I will lead the blind by a road they do not know, by paths they have not known I will guide them. I will turn the darkness before them into light, the rough places into level ground. These are the things I will do, and I will not forsake them." (Isaiah 42:16) Friend, THAT is the "new thing" we can look forward to! Our darkness will become light. The rough places smoothed. God is going to purify us as his Bride and restore us back to what he always intended us to be.

Feelings, experiences, visions, prophesies, and doctrines must always agree with God's written Word. If it does not, then the Bible says to reject it: "I urge you, brothers and sisters, to keep your eyes on those who cause dissensions and create obstacles or introduce temptations [for others] to commit sin, [acting in ways] contrary to the doctrine which you have learned. Turn away from them." (Romans 16:17 AMP)

3. Things have to line up with God's nature and character.

By reading the Bible for ourselves, we get to know the revealed nature and character of God, such as God is sovereign, living and true. He is life and the source of all life. He is immortal, infinite and eternal. God is loving, just and fair. He is merciful, gracious and good. He is truthful and faithful. God wants to heal, restore, reconcile, deliver, and set people free from bondage.

God also feels emotion. When you grieve, he grieves. When you rejoice, he rejoices with you. He walks with you through the ups and downs of life, "(3) Blessed [gratefully praised and adored] be the God and Father of our Lord Jesus Christ, the Father of mercies and the God of all comfort, (4) who comforts and encourages us in every trouble so that we will be able to comfort and encourage those who are in any kind of trouble, with the comfort with which we ourselves are comforted by God." (2 Corinthians 1:3-4 AMP)

"He was despised and rejected by men, A Man of sorrows and pain and acquainted with grief; And like One from whom men hide their faces He was despised, and we did not appreciate His worth or esteem Him." (Isaiah 53:3 AMP)

4. Test all teaching for sound doctrine, and test all lives for the fruit of the Spirit.

"Beloved, do not believe every spirit, but test the spirits to see whether they are from God; for many false prophets have gone out into the world." (1 John 4:1)

How do we test the spirits? By comparing what is being taught to Scripture and evaluating if the person is living in the fruit of the Spirit. We should also test our own words and actions to be sure we are in truth. (Galatians 6:4)

How much are we supposed to test? Everything. "But test all things carefully [so you can recognize what is good]. Hold firmly to that which is good." (1 Thessalonians 5:21)

By reading the Bible for yourself, you will know if what someone tells you stands the test of Scripture. No prophet, no husband, no pastor has the freedom to reinvent God's Word. The Bible will stand strong through time - it will never fail us. It is a rock that will keep us safe in turbulent times. God will defend his Word and your choice to follow him. Reading from your Bible every day and conversing with him builds a relationship that will carry you through difficult times, difficult relationships and opposition.

5. Take into consideration the historical, cultural and literary background.

The University of St. Thomas has an informative section on biblical exegesis. Part of that is examining the background of the writer and the context:

What can be known of the historical situation prior to and during the time the biblical book was written? How did society function at that time, e.g., what was the status of women, children, or slaves in the culture, what religions existed at the time of writing, or what were the main cultural values in society? What other texts might be like the book that contains your passage from the same time period? Are there other texts that might help you understand your passage? The Bible did not float down from heaven untouched by human hands. Rather, it was written over a long period of time, by real people. Who lived in real homes, with real families in real cultures. (8)

<u>6. Last, but not least, you are not inferior because you are a woman!</u>

"There is [now no distinction in regard to salvation] neither Jew nor Greek, there is neither slave nor free, there is neither male nor female; for you [who believe] are all one in Christ Jesus [no one can claim a spiritual superiority]." (Galatians 3:28 AMP)

I want to close with what Kyle Butt, M.Div., clarifies the actual biblical view of women is in contrast to popular opinion:

> The militant skeptical community incessantly attempts to discredit the Bible and the God Who is represented in its pages. One line of reasoning used in their efforts is to demand that the Bible presents a sexist picture of men and women, in which God and the Bible writers place more value on men, and view women as inferior and of less inherent worth. This accusation falls apart, however, when the entirety of the text is considered. Careful study reveals that Bible writers personified and illustrated such invaluable attributes as wisdom in the form of a woman. God himself compares traits that He possesses to similar traits found in women. Both the Old and New Testaments are filled with narratives lauding the actions of faithful, powerful women. The apostle Paul, who is often accused of misogyny, makes one of the boldest statements of gender equality ever recorded in religious literature. And the misguided attempt to discredit Paul by claiming that different gender roles in his epistles prove he valued women less cannot honestly or reasonably be sustained. In truth, the Bible presents the clearest picture of gender equity, value, and inherent worth ever recorded in either ancient or modern literature. The status of women in the Holy Scriptures, not only is not a challenge to its divine inspiration, but the biblical treatment of women actually provides another piece of evidence for the Bible's perfection and inspiration. (9)

Now that we have built a biblical foundation for correctly interpreting the Word of God, we can examine what it says about headship and submission.

Chapter Three
Headship and Submission in a Christian Marriage

Male headship sets the stage for domestic violence. I don't subscribe to that in any way, shape, or form. When we talk about a man and a woman in the sacrament of matrimony, we're talking about a partnership, people working together. One partner is just as much the expression of God's creation as the other.
Father Michael McDermott, Catholic Priest and Pastor of Saints Peter and Paul Church

Let's look at some scriptures that are often used to enforce marital control and submission, and how a growing number of theologians interpret them. When I first began discovering these truths, I felt like I had found a brand new priceless treasure! Finally, the Word of God was lining up with the nature and character I knew of him - a God of love, compassion and concern. The Bible began to make so much more sense and my relationship with God budded and grew like an eager new plant.

Of course, none of this is actually new. It has been God's intention all along. But my understanding of it was new, and the old lies I believed dropped away, bringing me freedom, peace and joy. This is by no means an exhaustive study. I just want to share with you a different perspective from respected theologians and leaders that you may not have been exposed to before. Then you can take what you learn here, study it further, and most importantly, allow this to start a conversation between you and God.

For your convenience, I first wrote out all the verses referred to, followed by the interpretations. Unless otherwise noted, I use the New Revised Standard Version, although the people I quote may use a different version.

1 Corinthians 7:4 "For the wife does not have authority over her own body, but the husband does; likewise the husband does not have authority over his own body, but the wife does."

1 Peter 2:13 "For the Lord's sake accept the authority of every human institution, whether of the emperor as supreme…"

1 Peter 3:1-7 "(1) Wives, in the same way, accept the authority of your husbands, so that, even if some of them do not obey the word, they may be won over without a word by their wives' conduct, (2) when they see the purity and reverence of your lives. (3) Do not adorn yourselves outwardly by braiding your hair, and by wearing gold ornaments or fine clothing; (4) rather, let your adornment be the inner self with the lasting beauty of a gentle and quiet spirit, which is very precious in God's sight. (5) It was in this way long ago that the holy women who hoped in God used to adorn themselves by accepting the authority of their husbands. (6) Thus Sarah obeyed Abraham and called him lord. You have become her daughters as long as you do what is good and never let fears alarm you. (7) Husbands, in the same way, show consideration for your wives in your life together, paying honor to the woman as the weaker sex, since they too are also heirs of the gracious gift of life—so that nothing may hinder your prayers."

Colossians 3:19 "Husbands, love your wives and never treat them harshly."

Ephesians 4:1-3 "(1) I therefore, the prisoner in the Lord, beg you to lead a life worthy of the calling to which you have been called, (2) with all humility and gentleness, with patience, bearing with one another in love, (3) making every effort to maintain the unity of the Spirit in the bond of peace."

Ephesians 5:21-33 "(21) Be subject to one another out of reverence for Christ. (22) Wives, be subject to your husbands as you are to the Lord. (23) For the husband is the head of the wife just as Christ is the head of the church, the body of which he is the Savior. (24) Just as the church is subject to Christ, so also wives ought to be, in everything, to their husbands. (25) Husbands, love your wives, just as Christ loved the church and gave himself up for her, (26) in order to make her holy by cleansing her with the washing of water by the word, (27) so as to present the church to himself in splendor, without a spot or wrinkle or anything of the kind—yes, so that she may be holy and without blemish. (28) In the same way, husbands should love their wives as they do their own bodies. He who loves his wife loves himself. (29) For no one ever hates his own body, but he nourishes and tenderly cares for it, just as Christ does for the church, (30) because we are members of his body. (31) "For this reason a man will leave his father and mother and be joined to his wife, and the two will become one flesh." (32) This is a great mystery, and I am applying it to Christ and the church. (33) Each of you, however, should love his wife as himself, and a wife should respect her husband."

Ezekiel 34:2-4 "(2) Mortal, prophesy against the shepherds of Israel: prophesy, and say to them—to the shepherds: Thus says the Lord God: Ah, you shepherds of Israel who have been feeding yourselves! Should not shepherds feed the sheep? (3) You eat the fat, you clothe yourselves with the wool, you slaughter the fatlings; but you do not feed the sheep. (4) You have not strengthened the weak, you have not healed the sick, you have not bound up the injured, you have not brought back the strayed, you have not sought the lost, but with force and harshness you have ruled them."

James 4:7 "Submit yourselves therefore to God. Resist the devil, and he will flee from you."

Jeremiah 23:1-4 "(1) Woe to the shepherds who destroy and scatter the sheep of my pasture! says the LORD. (2) Therefore thus says the LORD, the God of Israel, concerning the shepherds who shepherd my people: It is you who have scattered my flock, and have driven them away, and you have not attended to them. So I will attend to you for your evil doings, says the LORD. (3) Then I myself will gather the remnant of my flock out of all the lands where I have driven them, and I will bring them back to their fold, and they shall be fruitful and multiply. (4) I will raise up shepherds over them who will shepherd them, and they shall not fear any longer, or be dismayed, nor shall any be missing, says the LORD."

Mark 10:42-45 "(42) So Jesus called them and said to them, 'You know that among the Gentiles those whom they recognize as their rulers lord it over them, and their great ones are tyrants over them. (43) But it is not so among you; but whoever wishes to become great among you must be your servant, (44) and whoever wishes to be first among you must be slave of all. (45) For the Son of Man came not to be served but to serve, and to give his life a ransom for many.'"

Let's start with how the Rev. Dr. Marie Fortune interprets headship and submission passages in her book, *Keeping the Faith: Questions and Answers for the Abused Woman*:

> Question: The Bible says that the wife must submit to her husband. Does this mean that I must submit to his abuse?
>
> Actually, the scriptural passage that refers to the husband-wife relationship begins by saying: "Be subject to one another out of reverence for Christ." (Ephesians 5:21) This is the starting point for all our relationships as Christians, inside the family or outside. Here the words "be subject to" also mean "accommodate to" or "give way to." This means that we should all, including husbands and wives, seek to be flexible with each other and give way to each other.
>
> In another passage we find further clarification: "Let each of you look not only to his own interests, but also to the interests of others." (Philippians 2:4) So we are all, regardless of our relationship to each other, to be concerned for the other's welfare as well as for our own.
>
> Then scripture proceeds to specific reference to husbands and wives: "Wives, be subject to your husbands, as to the Lord. For the husband is the head of the wife as Christ is the head of the church, his body, and is himself its Savior." (Ephesians 5:22-23) This means that there are times in a Christian marriage when a wife should give way to her husband and recognize his interests as well as her own. But the husband's headship suggested here does not mean a role of unquestioned authority to which you are to be blindly obedient. What is described here is a model based on Christ's relationship to the church: Jesus was the servant of all who followed him, and he gave himself up for them. Never did he order people around, threaten, hit, or frighten them.
>
> Almost all the rest of this passage from Ephesians spells out the instructions to the husband in his treatment of his wife: he is to be to her as Christ was to the church. This means he is to serve her needs and be willing to sacrifice himself for her if need be. This is what Jesus did for the church. He is to love his

wife as himself, to nourish and cherish her. Another passage is even more specific: "Husbands, love your wives, and do not be harsh with them." (Colossians 3:19)

Clearly, the emphasis Scripture places on instructing husbands to care for and respect their wives just as Christ did the church leaves no room for excusing a husband's violent and abusive behavior toward his wife. (10)

ALL believers are called to mutual respect and submission to each other, *especially* husbands and wives. Paul, by using the example of the relationship between Christ and the church, automatically dispels warped ideas of each partner's role in marriage. No tyrannical husband can claim to be living a Christian marriage. There is absolutely no justification for anything less than kindness, respect and sacrificial love for each other.

Jesus wasn't married, but if he was, can you picture him treating his wife as your husband treats you? Jesus is our perfect example and he would never hurt or dominate you. Your husband has no biblical justification for doing it either.

Dr. Steven Tracy Ph.D., Professor of Theology and Ethics at Phoenix Seminary, says that the submission passage in Ephesians is actually focused on the behavior of husbands rather than wives:

> It is tragically ironic that Paul's submission command to wives in Ephesians 5:24 has often been used against wives to condone or justify harsh and abusive behavior by husbands. The focus in this paragraph (quantitatively and qualitatively) is overwhelmingly on husbands. In Ephesians 5:21-33, Paul uses a mere forty-seven words to admonish wives, but one hundred and forty-three words to admonish husbands. Even more importantly, Paul raises the bar for husbands as high as it could possibly be raised by commanding them to love their wives as Christ loved the church and gave himself for her. This is surely the loftiest, most demanding command given to husbands in the entire Bible.
>
> But Paul does not leave the reader simply with a sweeping and lofty *imitatio* Christi injunction. He elaborates on several specifics of Christ's costly sacrifice for the church and then in 5:28-29 again admonishes husbands to love their wives as Christ loved the church and again elaborates on the application. Paul

weaves a rich metaphor into this command by instructing husbands to love their wives as their own bodies, tenderly nourishing and cherishing them just as Christ tenderly cares for and nourishes his body the church.

Paul then finishes this paragraph by noting the mysterious sacred "one flesh" intimacy of marriage which pictures Christ's union with the church. Thus, if Ephesians 5:24 is understood in its context, selfish mistreatment of wives by husbands is utterly precluded. In fact, this passage makes such selfish manipulations by dominating husbands a slanderous assault on Christ, for marriage is to be a most winsome picture to the world of Christ's love and care for his bride. (11)

Before Brian and I married, we agreed to not have sexual relations until marriage because of the biblical mandate to wait until then. Brian was especially adamant about this, and I thought it was sweet of him to be so respectful of me and God's will. Boy was I fooled. It was just part of an image he wanted me to see.

After marriage, Brian required sex several times a day whether I wanted it or not. He would just show up and do what he wanted, ignoring my growing reluctance. Once I asked him why he thought he had a right to it so often, without my willing participation. His answer was matter-of-fact: "Because I am your husband and you have to submit to me whenever I want it." And that was that. It didn't matter that I was exhausted from raising a baby, or unenthusiastic at the monotony of several quickies a day. He was my husband and my role was to submit regardless of my personal feelings.

It was also a type of "payment" to him for being able to stay home full time with our children. I felt guilty because I secretly felt like a prostitute having to earn her room and board. I learned after I left Brian that this is actually real and a type of "passive prostitution."

Toward the end of our marriage, I told him "no" one day when he showed up and pushed me toward the bed. I was sick and very worried about catching a disease from him. He grabbed me and pushed me toward the bed again. I pulled back and said "NO, not this time." Without saying a word, he grabbed me and forced me onto the bed and had his way.

I remember feeling incredibly violated and broken at that moment. But it didn't make sense to me why I would feel that way, since he was my husband right? Husbands can't rape their wives! Then why did I feel raped? Why did I feel violated, used and worthless, and feel like my spirit was dying inside me? I slipped further into depression and hopelessness after that incident.

My feelings didn't subside, even though I pretended everything was normal. In fact, right after that incident, he demanded I take pictures of him showing off his muscles. My life felt so low and painful. Intertwined in this was his "spiritual speak." Everything felt confusing and conflicting.

Shortly after that while he was at work, I called a shelter and spoke with the Director of it. I hesitatingly shared with her some of what was happening and asked her if she thought I was going crazy. Her response changed my life. She said, "Robin, you have been raped. Your feelings are normal and expected of someone who has been raped. Marriage does not give anyone the right to force themselves on their spouse. That isn't love. That is breaking the law."

I will never forget the overwhelming relief I felt at being listened to and validated. To find out that I wasn't crazy! My feelings were normal! To people who have not endured abuse in an intimate relationship, this sounds far-fetched. Only those who have experienced this know what I am talking about - the crazy making, the emotional roller coasters, the depth of fear and despair that never seems to end. The Director helped me to see the truth of what was happening - I was in an abusive relationship. It wasn't my imagination and our relationship wasn't getting better.

This conversation with her was a crucial part of my journey to freedom. That is why I encourage women who feel confused about their relationship to talk to advocates at a shelter. Just one conversation can shed light into a dark world.

Leslie Vernick, a licensed clinical social worker and relationship coach, also insists on using correct terminology in her book *The Emotionally Destructive Relationship: Seeing It, Stopping It, Surviving It*:

> Submission is a discipline of the heart for all believers to practice, not just wives or women. All Christians are called to submit to authority (1 Peter 2:13), to one another (Ephesians 5:21), and to God (James 4:7). Please don't misunderstand what submission is and what it is not. In the Greek, the word submission (hupotasso) describes a voluntary action or attitude. Biblical submission cannot be forced. It is a position we take when we are motivated by our love for Christ and our de-

sire to please and obey him. Although God commands us to submit to him, obey him, and love him, he never forces anyone to comply with his commands. He gives us a free choice, including freedom to choose badly (like Adam and Eve did).

When a husband bullies his wife, his behavior does not describe biblical headship, nor is her forced "submission" characteristic of biblical submission. The correct terms are coercion, manipulation, intimidation, or rape and she is the victim. Let's make sure we use the right words. [Emphasis mine]

I am amazed in those instances when a man who believes so strongly in forcible submission is confronted with his own sin but is unwilling to submit himself to anyone else's authority for help and accountability, including his own pastor. He is not open to correction, challenge, or change because he is always right. He manipulates the Scriptures to serve his purposes.

Jesus cautions those in positions of authority—parents, husbands, pastors, and elders—not to misuse those God-ordained positions for self-centered purposes. These roles are given to us by God to humbly serve the individuals or groups that have been entrusted to our care, not to have our egos stroked or to get our own way. (Mark 10:42-45)

Sadly, some husbands have used their God-given position in their homes for selfish purposes, and often other Christians have unwittingly endorsed them. These husbands believe that they have license to do or demand anything they want, and that their wives are supposed to comply. This ought not to be. (12)

J. Lee Grady, an ordained minister and activist against abuse of women, explains in his article *The Dark Side of Wives Submitting to Husbands* that headship was never given as a license to control:

Marriage is not a hierarchy. Traditionalists assume that a Christian marriage is defined as a dominant husband who makes all family decisions while the wife graciously obeys without input. Yet Scripture actually portrays marriage as a loving partnership and refers to the wife as a "fellow heir of the grace of life." (1 Peter 3:7, NASB) And the apostle Paul taught that in the realm of sexuality, husbands and wives share equal authority over each other's bodies. (1 Corinthians 7:4) In other words, sub-

> mission in this most intimate part of a marriage covenant is mutual, and this same mutuality is the key to any happy marriage; it fosters respect, communication and an enduring bond.
>
> Headship is not a license to control. Traditionalists also cite Ephesians 5:23 to remind wives that their husbands are their "heads" - and they believe this term requires some type of dictatorial control in marriage. Yet the Greek word used in this passage, kephale, does not have anything to do with heavy-handed authority, and it cannot be used to enforce male domination. Neither does it imply male superiority. The word can either mean "source" (as in the source of a river) or "one who leads into battle" (as a protector).
>
> Neither original definition of this word gives room for abuse. Headship, in its essence, is not about who's the boss. Rather, it refers to the Genesis account of Eve being taken from Adam's side. The husband is the "source" of the wife because she originated from him, and she is intimately connected to him in a mystical union that is unlike any other human relationship.
>
> Men who abuse their wives are out of fellowship with God. First Peter 3:7 is clear: "You husbands in the same way, live with your wives in an understanding way, as with someone weaker, since she is a woman; and show her honor as a fellow heir of the grace of life, so your prayers will not be hindered."
>
> Wife abuse is no trivial sin. Any man who berates his wife, treats her as inferior or engages in abusive behavior (including hitting, kicking, raping, cursing at or threatening punishment) will jeopardize his fellowship with the Lord. He will feel frustrated and convicted until he repents. (13)

Many abusive men hide under the disguise of Christianity, and make a big deal of Ephesians 5 and similar passages. But the fact is that these very Scriptures condemn him. Abusers hate the truth revealed in these passages for they command him to love, serve and give himself up for his wife. That completely goes against his true nature and character, which is to dominate her.

Mary Kassian, distinguished professor of Women's Studies at Southern Baptist Seminary, in her article *7 Misconceptions about Submission* says:

> A husband does not have the right to demand or extract submission from his wife. Submission is HER choice - her responsibility... it is NOT his right!! Not ever. She is to "submit herself" - deciding when and how to submit is her call. In a Christian marriage, the focus is never on rights, but on personal responsibility. It's his responsibility to be affectionate. It's her responsibility to be agreeable. The husband's responsibility is to sacrificially love as Christ loved the Church - not to make his wife submit...
>
> A Christian's first responsibility is to submit to the Lord and His standard of righteousness. A wife is not called to submit to sin, mistreatment, or abuse. The Lord does not want "weak-willed" women - women who lack the discernment and strength to respond to the right things and in the right way. Godly women do not submit to sin. They carefully and intentionally weigh and discern how to submit to sinful human authority in light of their primary responsibility to submit to the ways of the Lord. No brain-dead doormats or spineless bowls of Jello here! Submission is neither mindless nor formulaic nor simplistic. Submitting to the Lord sometimes involves drawing clear boundaries and enacting consequences when a husband sins. Submission is an attitude of the heart. A woman can have a submissive spirit even when saying "no" and refusing to go along with sin. (14)

Biblical headship does not remove his wife's right to choose. At the heart of domestic violence and abuse is the sinful use of a husband's power to gain control over his wife. How does that align with sacrificial servant hood? Just like Leslie Vernick stressed: use proper terminology! A husband demanding his own way and mistreating his wife is not biblical headship. It's selfishness and abuse of power, and condemned by God.

What causes a man to treat his wife in this way? Brenda Branson and Paula Silva explain it in their book *Violence Among Us: Ministries to Families in Crisis*:

> An attitude of superiority and a deep disrespect for women, combined with feelings of entitlement and desire for power and control, prevent the abusive man from feeling empathy or compassion toward his wife. He feels little or no remorse when

he slaps her around because in his eyes she is always wrong; she is the one to blame. His goal is to discredit her, to silence her protests, and to divert attention from his bad behavior to her failures.

Where do these attitudes originate? They typically result from 1) male role models in the home who disrespect or abuse women; 2) cultural attitudes toward women as servants or property; and 3) distortion of Scripture preached from pulpits of all denominations for generations, erroneously teaching that because God created Adam first, man must be superior to woman in every way - mentally, physically, and spiritually. The colloquial corruption of the King James Version's 'help meet' in Genesis 2:18 into the so-called "helpmate" of tradition has been the source of many disrespectful attitudes toward women by Christian men. God does not give husbands the right to control or punish their wives... Other Scripture passages about submission (such as Ephesians 5:21-32) have been distorted by abusive men against their wives. They ignore the foundation of submission...where husbands are instructed to love their wives as Christ loved the church.

What does that love and leadership look like? Christ's love did not exploit, exert power and control, intimidate, demean, verbally abuse, or use force or violence... He did not demand his rights. Instead, He humbled Himself as a servant and washed the disciples' feet. "Submission is not a right given to a husband to demand but a precious gift given willingly by a woman 'as unto the Lord' (Ephesians 5:22). When an abusive, power-hungry man demands submission as his right, it is no longer a loving gift but a stolen treasure gained by extortion and coercion. (15)

Do you wonder if submission will change your husband? Debi Pryde and Robert Needham in their book *A Biblical Perspective of What to do When you are Abused by Your Husband* address this:

An abuse victim may think 'If I submit to this mistreatment with a loving and good attitude, God will help me and intervene.' But submitting to unjustified, impermissible evil is never blessed or righteous, not the least because it means the abuser is reinforced in his habituated wickedness, as well as being passively encouraged to lose out on God's intended blessings promised to husbands who cherish their wives.

Being persecuted for righteousness' sake (ie, our confession of Christ and our walk with Him) does not obligate us to passively receive or to submit to evil without resistance, but rather, the Scripture obligates us to overcome evil, actively. To be unwilling to expose a husband's abusive behavior is actually a profound lack of Christ-like love toward him and a selfish putting of one's own short-term safety ahead of his long-term spiritual good. (16)

God is good. He is a good Father who cherishes his daughters and does not want them to live sub-par inferior lives. You are meant for so much more than this! You are valuable and precious and have a God-given purpose in life. Don't let the enemy work through abusive men to keep you from fulfilling what God has called you to.

I remember one day, about two or three months before I left Brian, he was very angry with me. I don't remember the exact issue now, but we were standing in the kitchen in a sort of impasse. What I do remember very clearly is this: Brian finally stood still and stared at me speechless. I stared back quietly, unsure of what was coming next.

Finally, he resignedly shook his head. "You know what Robin? That's one thing I have never been able to figure out about you." He held up his thumb in front of my face then jammed it down on the counter top. "Every time I get you under my thumb, you crawl out. I can never get you to stay under my thumb." He shook his head at me as if I was a hopelessly naughty and willful child, and then walked off.

I thought to myself, wow - did he really just say that out loud? Is that really his goal? To break my spirit and gain total control over me? It was an eye-opening moment. This supposedly spiritual man hiding behind all this biblical gibberish and superiority was really just trying to break my spirit and gain complete control of me. He wanted me to submit and stay under his thumb. I felt stunned by the confession and committed to never letting anyone break my spirit.

Remember the definition Dr. Jeanne King gave for a true abuser: "The criteria for intimate partner violence consists of: possessiveness, controlling behavior, lack of empathy, externalization of blame, isolation of victimized partner, and the use of battering to create and maintain a relationship of unequal power."

That described Brian. I began referring to him in my mind as "The Thumb" to continually remind myself of his motive. His motive wasn't love. It was control, plain and simple. I never let him completely break me, even though he came close to it many times. Somehow, I always got back up and kept quietly fighting inside for my daughters and myself.

Pastor Jeff Crippen shares a helpful perspective on the perceived normalcy of abuse in his sermon *Bow Down, Tremble, and Pay Homage*:

> It is not normal in the Christian life to sin against someone, especially in an obvious, plain way (like abuse), and then be able to function without a violated conscience. To be able to go day after day without the thing weighing upon your conscience. To be able to sleep like a baby who has just thrown his oatmeal in his mother's face. This is NOT Christ. This is NOT the Spirit of Christ. You may have grown so accustomed to abuse that you think it is normal, and if the abuser professes to be a Christian, you may believe that this kind of thing is normal Christianity. You may be insistent that others accept you and the abuser 'just as you are' - because you have lived in the darkness so long that you do not recognize light (if you are a victim). And if you are the abuser, you believe that such evil is compatible with being a Christian. It is not.
>
> 1 John 4:20-21 ESV "(20) If anyone says, "I love God," and hates his brother, he is a liar; for he who does not love his brother whom he has seen cannot love God whom he has not seen. (21) And this commandment we have from him: whoever loves God must also love his brother."
>
> An abuser almost never does anything that he himself considers morally unacceptable. He may hide what he does because he thinks other people would disagree with it, but he feels justified inside…an abuser's core problem is that he has a distorted sense of right and wrong.
>
> And therefore, we say it once more - the abusive person, the person characterized by a profound sense of entitlement to power and control, by profound justification for the evil he uses to obtain that power and control - is not a Christian despite an ability to offer "wonderful" prayer, to expound upon accurate biblical doctrine, to be even an apparent model of Christianity. Because he fails THE ultimate test of Christ - that

he love Christ and that he love others. Satan appears as an "angel" of "light."

Matthew 23:13-15 ESV 13 "But woe to you, scribes and Pharisees, hypocrites! For you shut the kingdom of heaven in people's faces. For you neither enter yourselves nor allow those who would enter to go in. 15 Woe to you, scribes and Pharisees, hypocrites! For you travel across sea and land to make a single proselyte, and when he becomes a proselyte, you make him twice as much a child of hell as yourselves." (17)

As we have been learning, the issue of "submission" is not the problem. It is the way it is being interpreted that is causing strife in marriages. There is a huge difference between submissive love given freely from the heart, and coerced love by threats, abuse and ungodliness.

Men who are power-hungry and control oriented will misuse Scripture to get what they want. They take pieces of Scripture and twist it to serve their own selfish desires. God intends for us to read and interpret Scripture in context. We should be embracing the whole Bible, not just bits and pieces of it. If abusers would read their favorite Bible verses in context, they would lose their justification for what they do. There is no getting around that believers in Christ are to be "imitators of God," walking in love. Any other doctrine is false. "(1) Therefore be imitators of God, as beloved children, (2) and live in love, as Christ loved us and gave himself up for us, a fragrant offering and sacrifice to God." (Ephesians 5:1-2)

Here is a summary of Pastor Mark Hallock's sermon *God's Design for Wives* (based on Ephesians 5:22-24). In it he shares seven things that biblical submission do NOT mean:

1. That the wife is in any way inferior to, or less than, her husband.

2. That the wife becomes a passive participant in the marriage.

3. Putting the husband in the place of Christ as if the husband is some sort of absolute authority…therefore, it does not mean putting the will of the husband before the will of Christ. This means that if the husband tells his wife to do something that is against the will of God, or contrary to the bible, she can say "no."

4. Agreeing with everything her husband says and giving up independent thought.

5. That a wife gets her personal, spiritual strength from her husband. Rather, she gets her strength from God.

6. That a wife should give up her efforts to influence, guide, and help her husband be conformed to the image of Jesus. She can pray for him to be the leader God wants him to be.

7. Living in fearful intimidation of a husband who can strike out in physical, emotional, or spiritual abuse at any point. (18)

I want to encourage you if you are struggling with feelings that there is no hope and you might as well give up. You may feel that life will never get better and that you don't deserve better. Or _____ (you fill in the blank). DON'T GIVE UP! Your children need you to stay strong and keep fighting. There are others who will need your encouragement and support to help them through their pain. There is a purpose in all the pain you are experiencing. God has a plan for you. I hope that these excerpts from various pastors and leaders are helping you to see that God does not require you to endure a dangerous abusive relationship. In the next chapter, you will see that God offers concessions for getting out of these relationships. There is hope that all this pain you are experiencing will end WITH God's blessing!

In closing, I would like to share Dr. Steven Tracy's six principles regarding the parameters of female submission:

> 1. A wife must not submit to her husband when obedience to him would violate a biblical principle (not just a direct biblical statement).
>
> All but the most extreme fundamentalists agree that a wife should not obey her husband if it involves violating a direct command of Scripture. But many moral issues wives face today are not directly addressed in Scripture (internet pornography, in vitro fertilization, gambling, cosmetic surgery, abortion, sexual fetishes, etc.). If we accept the doctrine of the sufficiency of Scripture, then we must not restrict a woman's right to refuse to submit to her husband to those instances in which she can cite a direct biblical statement that contradicts her husband's command... Often a wife may not be able to point to a specific biblical text to justify her objection to her husband's

command but will only be able to appeal to her sense of the broad teachings of Scripture which she truly believes are applicable to the issue at hand.

2. A wife must not submit to her husband when obedience to him would compromise her relationship with Christ.

We have noted that Christ, not a husband, is a Christian wife's supreme Lord. She is Christ's bride first and foremost. The early Christian apostles were commanded by their religious authorities to quit teaching about Christ. Their response is instructive: "We must obey God rather than men" (Acts 5:29)…Modern Christian wives must recognize that their first allegiance is to Christ. Their husband is neither their priest nor their lord…Hence, a husband has no right to dictate his wife's relationship with Christ. In practical terms this means a wife should not obey her husband if he tells her not to go to church or to a Bible study, forbids her from going to a counselor, pastor, or Christian advisor, or forbids her from spending time with a trusted friend.

3. A wife must not submit to her husband when obedience to him would violate her conscience.

Sometimes a husband will order his wife to do something that she cannot identify as patently unbiblical, and yet the behavior is internally objectionable to her. That is, it would violate her conscience. Again, based on the fact that Christ is her Lord, and based on Paul's teaching that we must always act in faith before Christ and not violate our conscience (Romans 14:22-23), a wife should not obey a husband if doing so will violate her conscience. This principle is particularly helpful in our culture when a husband requests his wife to participate in sexual practices that she finds objectionable.

4. A wife must not submit to her husband when obedience to him would compromise the care, nurture, and protection of her children.

God calls adults to prioritize protecting and caring for the vulnerable, particularly children (Isaiah 1:17; Jeremiah 22:3). Care for the vulnerable, including children, is described as the purest form of religion (James 1:27). In Scripture, both fathers and mothers have a responsibility to care for their children physically and spiritually (Deuteronomy 6:4-7; Proverbs 31:10-31; Ephesians 2:7-8, 11-12). Thus, children are commanded to obey their fathers and their mothers (Proverbs 1:8; Ephesians 6:1)... We should particularly note that children innately develop their sense of God's character from their experience with their earthly father. So children whose fathers are abusive or harsh develop distorted views of their heavenly father. Thus, if a husband is harsh, verbally abusive, or uses excessive forms of punishment (including physical abuse), a wife has a moral obligation to protect the children regardless of her husband's requests or demands.

5. A wife must not submit to her husband when obedience to him would enable (facilitate) her husband's sin.

Not only are wives to avoid obeying a husband's command to sin, but they should also avoid following any commands that facilitate a husband's sin. The holiness of God requires that we not enable others to sin with greater ease

6. A wife must not submit to physical, sexual, or emotional abuse.

...It is thus important to recognize that enduring avoidable abuse, including at the hands of one's authorities, is not commended biblically. Scripture affirms the wisdom and propriety of fleeing an abuser, "a prudent man sees danger and takes refuge, but the simple keep going and suffer for it." (Proverbs 22:3) There are numerous biblical accounts of godly individuals who avoided physical abuse from their authorities (civic and religious) whenever possible... Not only is it entirely biblical for a wife to flee or otherwise refuse to submit to abuse of her and her children's physical and emotional wellbeing, but not submitting to an abusive husband is also best for the husband. Wives are to do good to their husbands (Proverbs 31:12), and one of the best ways wives of abusive husbands can do this is by challenging the abusive behavior through fleeing, filing assault charges, contacting church authorities, or by otherwise stimulating real accountability and painful consequences for the abusive behavior. Refusing to submit to abuse and instead taking action to not allow it to continue is good for the husband because: (1) this is one of the best ways to break through the abusers' distorted thinking and stimulate repentance; (2) It

> decreases the temporal and eternal consequences that accrue the longer a husband abuses. In cases of unrepentant abuse, divorce may well be a tragic necessity. (19)

God knew that some men would mistreat their wives and children. He knew that many would do it in his name, to justify their abuse and reinforce their assumed power and authority. So God did something very loving for you. He laid out what his perfect plan was for marriage, and then he laid out concessions so that victims of abuse could have a way out.

In the next chapter, we are going to look at these concessions. You probably know about two of them: abandonment and adultery. But there are actually more and they may apply to your situation.

Chapter Four
Escaping the Ultimate Loneliness

1. Abandonment
2. Adultery
3. Lust
4. Idolatry
5. Physical and Sexual Abuse
6. Fraud
7. Fear for Your Life
8. Passive Neglect

"If you don't have a deep love relationship in your marriage, then you have a fake marriage. It may look good to others, but it doesn't look good to God... [Christians] teach that marriage is a set of vows and roles and behaviors. The Bible teaches that husbands and wives are one, and equal in God's eyes, but we set the husband above the wife. We teach that marriage is the lack of divorce... We have leeched out the true meaning of marriage and supplanted it with a formula that will produce a stable system with no life... God created marriage so that there would not be loneliness... so that humans could be fulfilled in an ultimate relationship. But our recipe for marriage creates the ultimate loneliness."

Don Francisco, Christian Musician

"God Hates Divorce!" "Divorce is Sin!" We hear that all the time don't we? By the time you finish this chapter, I hope you will view separation or divorce from a destructive relationship with a sense of God's love and compassion, rather than the condemnation and hopelessness that typically accompanies those statements.

Patriarchal religious leaders frequently counsel wives to provide to their husband the benefits of what would belong in a good marriage, but ignore the toxic environment he creates for her to perform those benefits in. They condemn any suggestion that she complain or even consider a divorce from what amounts to an impossible and hellish life.

Though they may not intend to be cruel, their ignorance of the Bible and of domestic abuse/violence causes them to thoughtlessly parrot what they have always been taught. Since they are not on the receiving end of abuse, they can't step out of their narrow and privileged perspective. They have no concept of what it is like to endure abuse. Therefore, it is easy for them to proclaim against the abused wife things like:

- Divorce is sin! YOU are breaking the marriage vows "'til death do us part."
- God said you cannot divorce for any reason!
- You and your husband are one for better or worse!
- Divorce is quitting! God never quits and you should be Christ-like.
- Divorce is your unwillingness to forgive and forget, so you must not even be a Christian!
- Divorce is self-righteous hypocrisy. You aren't perfect either!
- Only people who are selfish and prideful get a divorce!
- Divorce is open rebellion toward God, which is witchcraft!
- True love is unconditional. True love hangs in there no matter how bad it gets.
- Stay and Pray! God will reward your faithfulness in heaven.
- What God has joined, you must not divide! You will come under a curse if you do.
- God wanted you to marry him so that he would come to salvation because of your humble faithfulness.

Ironically, it is those who are supposed to bring spiritual light that actually condemn perpetrators, victims and their children to spiritual darkness.

Abused wives struggle in their relationship with God, feeling that he does not care and has distanced himself from them. Some abandon their faith entirely, not wanting to serve a God that apparently does not love them and condemns them and their children to suffer so terribly.

Abusers suffer also, because they are reinforced in their delusion that they are right and can act with impunity. They are helped along on their eternally destructive path by the very institution that is supposed to warn them of the consequences of their continued sin, and guide them toward right living and right standing with God.

How often children forsake anything having to do with God because of the religious hypocrisy they witnessed growing up.

The attitude behind most of these accusations and demands stem from an underlying bias that views control of women a right of men; an assumption that women are physically, mentally and spiritually inferior to men; and a distorted perception of God as Law Master and ally in the subjugation of women. This faulty belief system is found in many religions, and unfortunately, Christianity is not immune. God says clearly and repeatedly in the Bible how much he hates injustice and oppression of anyone.

When the above statements are said to an abused wife, it is nearly always said in a way that conveys SHE is the one who is selfish, unfaithful, self-centered and completely misaligned with God if she utters any unhappiness about her marriage. The husband's biblical responsibility is evaded, as if by very reason of having male DNA he is exempt from abiding by the law of love.

The biggest danger in these traditional religious interpretations is that they demand simplistic answers to the reality of insanely difficult and often dangerous relationships. They resist any moral imperative to act on behalf of the oppressed if the "oppressed" means they are female and have a wedding ring on. They ignore the majority of the Bible that demands mercy, protection and justice for victims. They conveniently protect patriarchal churches and leaders from controversy that may cause a loss in membership and dollars. Money, comfort and status, rather than moral excellence and truth, are still the driving force behind many religious leaders and organizations no matter how much they piously claim otherwise.

What is inarguable is that God really does hate divorce. However, the reasons God gives for it, and the reasons given by many religious leaders, are two different things. God hates divorce because it represents the failure of a man and woman to come together in the ultimate beautiful unity that he designed for their pleasure and fulfillment.

Divorce represents pain and heartache. It represents a failure to love. Whether one or both spouses fail to uphold the covenant, it does not matter. God doesn't care about gender. People are suffering in obvious and hidden ways, and that suffering breaks his heart, as it should ours. People are missing the joy and peace that he wanted them to experience in their relationship.

When domestic violence and abuse is present, everyone in the family loses: they lose their trust, security, happiness, safety, respect and love. Some will make it through and find a way to live a good life in spite of the scars. Others are forever changed by it, enduring a lifelong cycle of personal relational dysfunction and heartache.

The Bible also makes it clear that divorce was not a part of God's original plan for marriage. Common sense says that sin destroyed much of God's original plan for the human race, so he made concessions out of his love, mercy, grace and plan of redemption. Women are not exempt from these concessions. Abused wives are not exempt!

It appears that the only New Testament concessions for divorce are adultery (Matthew 5:31-32) or abandonment by an unbeliever (1 Corinthians 7:15). As discussed in chapter two, rightly interpreting Scripture requires not just regarding specific statements about the sanctity of marriage, but also the context, God-inspired exceptions, and a cultural understanding.

Don Francisco explains the often-misused verse of Malachi 2:16, "For I hate divorce, says the Lord, the God of Israel, and covering one's garment with violence, says the Lord of hosts. So take heed to yourselves and do not be faithless."

> Of course, marriages are intended to be lifelong. But in this imperfect world divorce can sometimes be lifesaving... The widely used verse in Malachi, where God seems to state that He "hates divorce" is mistranslated. What God hates is literally "the putting out" of a woman.
>
> Putting out is altogether different than divorce in Jewish culture. A man would permanently kick his wife out, denying her the Jewish divorce certificate. This woman would still be legally married, but with no home. Her dowry and children would be retained by the husband. She would have already surrendered her virginity to him. She would be ineligible to remarry, since technically, she was still legally bound to her husband. Further, her culture would label her as an adulteress since she did not have a valid divorce certificate. And this lady couldn't just rent an apartment and get a job teaching kindergarten - there was no place for a put out woman in Jewish culture of that day except prostitution. Since the marriages were most often arranged, this whole horrible chain of events would have been completely out of her control.
>
> The husband, however, was free to marry again and to do this as much as he liked. That is why Moses required a divorce cer-

tificate to be given... so that the marriage was legally, fairly, and religiously terminated and the woman would be free to remarry and go on with life... A Jewish divorce certificate is so valuable that often after a man puts out a woman, he will legally obtain the certificate and then sell it to the highest bidder...

All over the Bible we have ignorantly and clumsily translated "put out" as "divorce." This has caused many errant doctrines to be formed and made a terrible mess out of millions of people's lives. The toll in human suffering because of our ignorance is overwhelming. The Bible simply does not say that God hates divorce. It says that God hates the putting away.

In the New Testament, Jesus continues to address this cruel breach of human rights. Nearly all of the verses translated "divorce" in the Gospels actually say "put away." It is a completely different situation which we have no equivalent for. Knowing this makes a world of difference. For instance, many believe that Christian remarriage is adultery. But Jesus did not say that if a man marries a divorced woman, he would be committing adultery. He said that if a man married a "put out" woman, he would be committing adultery. This is because she was technically still married! In Israel, putting a woman out is a devastating, intentional ruination of a woman's life. God still hates it. (20)

This makes me think of Jesus coming to give us life: John 10:10 "The thief comes only to steal and kill and destroy. I came that they may have life, and have it abundantly." Jesus is talking about spiritual life and abundance. Look at the fruit of your pastor, your husband, and whoever else is telling you in so many words to shut up and submit.

If Jesus is behind the message, it will move you into a life of peace and harmony. If "the thief" is behind it, it will steal your peace and joy, and kill your spirit, your future, your dreams, your destiny. Primary to spiritual life is feeling safe, loved and respected in your own home. That is God's will for you - not control and domination.

Stephen Gola expounds on the Malachi passage in his book, *Divorce: God's Will?*:

> We have heard this Scripture: "the Lord God of Israel says that HE HATES DIVORCE" (Malachi 2:16). This is almost always quoted as if God hates all divorces in general. But that's just

not true... there are TWO "kinds" of marriages and TWO "divorces" being mentioned in the Malachi 2:11-16 passage.

The "divorces" were not official divorces; they didn't need to be. They were already previously married and "unofficially" married again. The Hebrew word shalach means "putting away" - a separation, as correctly translated in most Bibles. However, the King James and a number of newer versions have incorrectly translated shalach as to mean: divorce. It never meant divorce and it doesn't mean divorce. The word was most likely translated as "divorce" to fit what was taught in the church. Shalach is just a common word used throughout the Old Testament which means to: go, separate or to send. That's it!

So why did God angrily say that He "...hated putting away [a separation]?" "...Because you have not kept My ways [concerning marriage, divorce and remarriage] but have SHOWN PARTIALITY IN THE LAW" (Malachi 2:9). The Law specifically stated that when a man got a divorce from his wife that he was to write "...her a CERTIFICATE OF DIVORCE, put it in her hand, AND [shalach] send her out [put her away]..." (Deuteronomy 24:1)... Instead, men separated from their wives without ever giving them a Certificate of Divorce and then illegally married someone else. This is why the Lord said that they were still "their wife by covenant." The marriage covenant had never been dissolved by the Divorce Certificate.

The Lord's holy institution which He loves...the Lord has been witness between you and the wife of your youth...[and] SHE [STILL] IS YOUR COMPANION AND YOUR WIFE BY COVENANT. For the Lord God of Israel says that He hates divorce [shalach], [separating without a Certificate of Divorce]... Because these men had remarried illegally — separated from their wives without giving them a Certificate of Divorce, they were in adultery as Jesus stated: "Furthermore it has been said, "Whoever PUTS AWAY [separates from {apoluo}] his wife, LET HIM GIVE HER A CERTIFICATE OF DIVORCE. But I say to you that whoever PUTS AWAY [separates and remarries without being divorced from] his wife for any reason except sexual immorality causes her to commit adultery: and whoever marries a woman who is PUT AWAY [separated without being divorced {apoluo}] commits adultery" (Matthew 5:31-32). (The Lord never forgot about the Malachi incident when He came to earth to redeem lost man).

Because these disobedient men still had "un-divorced" wives, the Lord did not command them to give their illegal wives a Certificate of Divorce, rather, they simply had to "separate, put them away, [shalach]." SO DID GOD HATE DIVORCE? NO! RATHER, GOD HATED THAT THE HUSBANDS WERE SEPARATING FROM THEIR WIVES WITHOUT GIVING THEM A CERTIFICATE OF DIVORCE WHICH WOULD ENABLE THEM TO GET REMARRIED. THIS IS WHAT GOD HATES! (21)

Pastor Jeff Crippen addresses the hypocrisy of those who get angry at the suggestion an abused woman divorce her husband in his article *Marriage, Divorce, and an Ox in a Well*. The truth in this article made such an impression on me, that I am sharing it here in its entirety. I strongly encourage anyone who struggles with these issues to read Pastor Jeff's books and articles on *A Cry for Justice*.

> Luke 14:1-6 "(1) One Sabbath, when he went to dine at the house of a ruler of the Pharisees, they were watching him carefully. (2) And behold, there was a man before him who had dropsy. (3) And Jesus responded to the lawyers and Pharisees, saying, "Is it lawful to heal on the Sabbath, or not?" (4) But they remained silent. Then he took him and healed him and sent him away. (5) And he said to them, "Which of you, having a son or an ox that has fallen into a well on a Sabbath day, will not immediately pull him out?" (6) And they could not reply to these things."
>
> One of the prevalent dangers in the church - especially in the conservative, Bible-believing church like the one I pastor - is that of falling prey to wooden, literalistic interpretation of Scripture that totally misses the heart of God and thus the real spirit of a particular passage. The error is the same as the Pharisaical handling of the Scriptures Jesus confronted here. The day of Sabbath rest was turned into "no work is to be done on the Sabbath," and that included even works that showed mercy to those in need. Nope, can't eat on the Sabbath if you have to make a sandwich - you can just go hungry. Nope, can't heal someone.

Jesus took these knuckleheads to their own hypocrisy. If their son or even their oxen fell into a pit or a well on the Sabbath, what was their common response? "He will just have to stay there and perish. He should have picked one of the other six days to fall in there. Look, everyone, at how holy I am. I am so pious that I am even willing to let my son suffer or die rather than violate this Sabbath day." Ooooh. Aaaaah. Yeah, oh man, what a holy guy. Not! God's love and mercy and care for human beings and even animals does not cease on the Sabbath! He still feeds them and cares for them and yes, even pulls them out of a well if they fall in. The Lord of the Sabbath effects works of mercy on the day of rest.

Now here's the deal. Abuse victims are in a pit. Yes, God's intent is that marriage be a blessing. A life-long blessed covenant between a man and a woman. Love, honor, cherish - the whole thing. One flesh, self-sacrificing love. But sometimes it just isn't. Why? Because of sin. Because some husbands (and some wives) are just plain evil, cruel despots out to dominate and use and inflict pain. In other words, abuse victims have fallen into a pit.

So let me ask you this, Mr. or Mrs. preacher of "thou shalt never divorce for any reason, not even for abuse," what do you do when a dog is being cruelly treated by his master? A dog. Or a cat. Or a hamster. A horse. There the critter is, skin and bones out in the pasture. Starving. He knocks his water bucket over. Or the dog chews up a shoe (or commits some even more minor infraction like whining because he is hungry). You see the owner beating that animal and cursing it. Kicking it. Depriving it even more of food and water. Teasing and toying with it. What will you do?

Unless you are of the same ilk as that cruel master (and frankly, I believe that some of you people who mistreat abuse victims are indeed of the same ilk as the abuser), you will be reporting that cruelty to animals to the authorities and have that dog or horse or even a pet rodent rescued!! You will be calling for justice.

And so I ask you - no, no - JESUS CHRIST asks you, "which one of you, seeing a dog being beaten, will not rescue that dog

> from the 'covenant' of dog ownership?" The punch line almost need not even be stated, but here it is anyway:
>
> "If you are ready to rescue a dog from cruelty and bondage, why do you refuse to rescue a human being from the same? Why do you forbid divorce, denying it to people who are wickedly treated and persecuted by a spouse who does not and never has kept the marriage covenant?" Many of you who preach this no-divorce for abuse line are very loud voices when it comes to the righteous opposition to abortion. And yet, when that baby whom you are so zealous to protect from violence now becomes an adult and marries a wicked man, you leave them in bondage even if their life is in danger.
>
> God's mercy and kindness and His justice for the oppressed must never be sacrificed in our interpretation of His Word, else we join ranks with the Pharisees. Now go, and learn what God really requires. (22)

The truth is that religious leaders have an option. They can interpret Scripture with a heart that loves and cares about men and women equally. Or they can selfishly interpret Scripture to subjugate women. The Bible lists prominent and revered women leaders. Women held leadership roles in the early church. Nowhere in the Bible does God imply inferiority based on gender. It actually wasn't until the fourth century that men began to distort Scripture against the equality of women and toward male superiority. This is a man-made religious addendum, not an actual Biblical truth. Sadly, this has justified a pervasive abuse of women within the institution that claims to represent God's eternal truths. I can't imagine God is pleased to be represented in such a vile way.

Reverend Marie Fortune tackles the often used yet misquoted Matthew 19:6 verse in her book *Keeping the Faith: Questions and Answers for the Abused Woman*:

> "What therefore God has joined together, let no man put asunder." (Matthew 19:6) Any man who brings violence and abuse into his family life is putting asunder the marriage covenant that God has blessed. The violence is what breaks up the marriage, and the one responsible for that violence is the one responsible for the breakup. The actual divorce is in fact only

the public acknowledgment of the private truth that a marriage covenant has been long since destroyed by abuse.

"And this again you do. You cover the Lord's altar with tears, with weeping and groaning because (God) no longer regards the offering or accepts it with favor at your hand. You ask, "Why does (God) not?" Because the Lord was witness to the covenant between you and the wife of your youth, to whom you have been faithless, though she is your companion and your wife by covenant. Has not the one God made and sustained for us the spirit of life: And what does (God) desire? Godly offspring. So take heed to yourselves, and let none be faithless to the wife of his youth. "For I hate divorce." says the Lord the God of Israel, "and covering one's garment with violence" says the Lord of hosts. "So take heed to yourselves and do not be faithless." (Malachi 2:13-16)

We have always taught within the Christian tradition that the marriage covenant is broken by sexual unfaithfulness in marriage. The main reason that adultery is a problem is that it results in broken trust between husband and wife. But we should also realize that there are other kinds of unfaithfulness. Bringing violence into one's marriage is also unfaithfulness. Once violence has entered a relationship, trust is destroyed. If you can't trust your husband not to hit you, what can you trust? When God says in this passage that God hates divorce, God is acknowledging the pain that we all feel when a situation reaches the point where a divorce is necessary, when the brokenness is so great that it cannot be repaired. God does not say, "Thou shalt not divorce." But God grieves that unfaithfulness of any kind to the marriage covenant results in a divorce. (23)

I used to think a lot on the Matthew 19:6 verse of not dividing what God has joined. I really felt that God tried to warn me against marrying Brian, but I ignored it. I grew up believing that if you were married, God was the one who put the relationship together - thus the sin of divorce. But my experience with Brian didn't agree with that belief any longer. I knew I jumped into my marriage with Brian out of my own personal fears, desires and impulsiveness. I figured once I was in it, God would bless it because he had to right? Ultimately, he brought us together right? WRONG. To say that is to avoid personal responsibility and the fact that God does give people a free will. So, what if God doesn't join every marriage together?

Stephen Gola addresses the question of unsanctified marriages:

> We tend to think that EVERY marriage is blessed and seen as holy by God because of what we've been taught, but not every marriage is! God does not call holy that which is unholy. God desires us to be like Himself, to be able to "...distinguish between holy and unholy, and between unclean and clean" (Leviticus 10:10). If we do not have this discernment, we can make or continue in a fatal marriage. JUST BECAUSE WE ARE MARRIED BY THE LAW, IT DOESN'T MEAN THAT THE LAWGIVER HIMSELF HAS MARRIED US.
>
> Many people stay trapped for years in marriages that God will not bless. Many are abused slaves to their spouse. They cry out, "Why doesn't God bless our marriage?" Blessings are given to the person who will call upon Him, love Him, and put Him first. God does bless us as much as He can, but many times it falls far short of what we really need because we block God.
>
> Some unsanctified marriages… may have [husbands raping their wives, abuse, child sexual abuse, etc.] Some marriages have deteriorated over time, while others may have been bad from the start. Some unsanctified marriages may not have any outward manifestations of uncleanness at first. Some of the more common things that cause a marriage partner to be unclean are alcoholism, drugs, lustful sex, or a party spirit. The Bible has much to say about being a part of these things. Examples in the Bible are found in Ephesians 5:3-12, 1 Corinthians 6:9-11, and 1 Corinthians 5:1-13.
>
> People live and die without ever experiencing the blessings that God pronounces on a sanctified marriage. They feel trapped and so continue in abusive situations because of what they have been taught (or not taught). For example, you may have been taught that once you've been married you can never get a divorce because "God hates divorce", no matter how wrong, abusive, or unholy the marriage is.
>
> The truth is, God is more for the divorce than He is for the marriage. But He IS able to change a heart to stop the unclean

and unrighteous acts if that person will call out and yield their life totally to Him. (24)

Now we will look at eight things that break a marital covenant.

1. Abandonment

1 Corinthians 7:15 lists abandonment (desertion) as grounds for divorce. Abandonment is a violation of the covenant by abdicating pledged responsibilities inherent in most marriage vows.

Your husband may leave your home without lawful cause and refuse to return. As a matter of delinquency, he may stop providing for your care, protection or support, for example, if you have health problems or minor children. Abandonment is intentional non-support of the other spouse who is in destitute or necessitous circumstances, and is grounds for divorce.

There is also the flip side called constructive abandonment. In this way he may make your life so unbearable in your home that you have no other option but to leave. This might take the form of physical abuse or other acts that impair your health and make life intolerable. Or perhaps he changes the locks and prevents you from entering your home.

If he deliberately commits a crime, is convicted and sent to prison for a lengthy time - this may fall under the category of abandonment. He has knowingly placed himself in a position where it is possible he will no longer be able to fulfill his pledged marital responsibilities. However it occurs, he has abandoned you. God permits you to seek a divorce in this case.

> Pastor Jeff Crippen expounds on the concession of abandonment:
>
> "But if anyone does not provide for his relatives, and especially for members of his household, he has denied the faith and is worse than an unbeliever." (1 Timothy 5:8)
>
> Now, Paul says that anyone who does not provide for his relatives, especially for his own family, has done two things: (1) He has denied the gospel. In other words, he is a practical apostate, and (2) He has revealed that he is an unbeliever of the worst kind. Worst, because many people who don't even claim to be Christians nevertheless care for their own families...

> A true Christian is a new creation. He is indwelt by the Spirit of Jesus and taught by that Spirit. He is led by the Spirit and by the Spirit he puts to death the deeds of the flesh. Once a hater of God, he now loves God and loves God's Law. He does not need to be forced to love others, including his wife and children, and stop abusing them. If these things are not true of a person, then he is not a Christian at all...
>
> Because this single verse says everything. A man who does not provide for members of his own household has denied the faith (no matter how much God-talk he spews) and is the worst kind of unbeliever...
>
> We all know that all too frequently pressure is put upon abuse victims not to divorce their abuser. That is putting it mildly. They are frequently "forbidden" to divorce their abuser is more accurate. And one of the reasons given for this prohibition is that her husband "is a Christian" and she can only divorce (the claim goes) a spouse who is a non-believer and who doesn't agree to live together with her (1 Corinthians 7 normally cited and misused here).
>
> But check it out. Paul says that the abuser is WORSE than an unbeliever! He isn't just an unbeliever who is ignorant of the gospel. Oh no. He is a person who KNOWS about Christ, who has professed Christ, who has "tasted" (Hebrews 6) Christ. And yet, he spits in our Lord's face and tramples on our Lord's blood by his wicked treatment of his own household. So of course an abuse victim has the right before God to divorce such a person. (25)

2. Adultery

Matthew 5:32 is usually cited as the other concession for divorce. Dr. Chris Trotter, an author and senior lecturer in social work at Monash University, and Michael Clanchy, a writer and counselor, explain why adultery (infidelity) can be as abusive as being hit:

> Why is infidelity abusive? Why is it sometimes a form of psychological and emotional violence? Because infidelity can be as devastating as a violent attack. It results in humiliation, hurt and loss for the injured partner. The betrayal is usually per-

ceived as a direct attack on the faithful partner's worth as a person and as a partner.

A research project involving in-depth interviews with a number of women and men who have experienced infidelity has been conducted at Monash University. The stories reveal numerous parallels between certain cases of infidelity and cases of psychological and physical abuse. The research found that common characteristics of abuse and infidelity include:

- The Recurring Cycle. As with domestic violence, infidelity can become an ongoing feature of some relationships.

- Similar Phases. Ongoing infidelity sometimes follows a path similar to the well-documented domestic abuse cycle. A typical cycle might include a tension build-up phase, the infliction of pain, a brief period of remorse and guilt and then the reconciliation phase, followed by a return to tension build-up.

- Apparent Indifference of the Betraying Partner. Apart from brief periods of guilt and remorse after critical incidents of abuse or infidelity, the betrayers/abusers tend to be insensitive to the pain and distress they inflict on their partners. They often continue their infidelity or abuse without accepting responsibility for the anguish they cause.

- Similarity of the Responses of the Injured Parties. Those who stay for significant periods of time with partners who are unfaithful, often display the same psychological and social symptoms exhibited by victims of systematic abuse.

Some of these symptoms include deep personal suffering; low self-esteem and a sense of worthlessness; a sense of helplessness and a lack of control over their lives; a dependency on the betraying partner and a need for their approval; and a distorted sense of reality in which they can begin to believe that their partner's infidelity is their own fault.

Behaviour patterns established by partners in abuse and infidelity situations can be difficult to change. Like domestic violence, unfaithful behaviour does not often cease of its own accord, but calls for definitive action on the part of either the perpetrator, the affected party or both... Unfaithful behaviour is heavily associated with lies, deception and denial. (26)

As pointed out so clearly by the research project at Monash University, adultery is devastating to victims in numerous ways. Under Moses' law, the penalty for adultery was death, a serious consequence! (Leviticus 20:10) I love Jesus' response though, when he was challenged by the church leaders who were infuriated with a woman (not the man of course) caught in the act of adultery. His response was full of grace and wisdom: "When they kept on questioning him, he straightened up and said to them, 'Let anyone among you who is without sin be the first to throw a stone at her.'" (John 8:7)

No one could claim to be without sin except Jesus. After the woman's accusers left, Jesus kindly admonished her to accept his forgiveness and continue her life with character and integrity. God still hates adultery, but through Christ's sacrifice and atonement on the cross, men and women guilty of adultery can repent and receive grace and complete forgiveness.

How the innocent spouse chooses to respond to the revelation of adultery is his/her choice. Some choose to forgive a truly repentant spouse and move into a fulfilling and happy marriage. For others, trust is forever broken and repair of the relationship is impossible. Chapter six will give the signs of true repentance.

Not all adultery is abuse. It may be a symptom of a poor relationship that can be repaired. However, it may be just one more dynamic in an already abusive relationship.

Pastor Jeff Crippen shows how abuse and adultery is in fact desertion, and a concession for divorce:

> The victim of abuse, normally the wife but sometimes the husband, has a right before God to leave Egypt, to divorce the abuser. And I believe that anyone who comes to a true and proper understanding of the nature and tactics and evil of genuine abuse, will come to the same conclusion… I base my conclusion on 1 Corinthians 7:10-16 ESV:
>
> "10 To the married I give this charge (not I, but the Lord): the wife should not separate from her husband 11 (but if she does, she should remain unmarried or else be reconciled to her husband), and the husband should not divorce his wife. 12 To the rest I say (I, not the Lord) that if any brother has a wife who is an unbeliever, and she consents to live with him, he should not divorce her. 13 If any woman has a husband who is an unbeliever, and he consents to live with her, she should not divorce

him. 14 For the unbelieving husband is made holy because of his wife, and the unbelieving wife is made holy because of her husband. Otherwise your children would be unclean, but as it is, they are holy. 15 But if the unbelieving partner separates, let it be so. In such cases the brother or sister is not enslaved. God has called you[a] to peace. 16 For how do you know, wife, whether you will save your husband? Or how do you know, husband, whether you will save your wife?"

Now, have you ever given real thought to just what it means to consent to live with a husband or wife? Or what it means (v 15) to separate from a husband or wife? Far too many Christians, I believe, conclude and assume that this simply means - to not file formal, legal divorce proceedings and to not physically throw the victim out of the house. I think that is the kind of application, or rather MIS-application that the Pharisees were characterized by.

Consenting to live with my wife, not separating from my wife, means rather that I keep my wedding vows made before God and witnesses to love, honor, cherish my wife. To live out a one-flesh relationship with her. To love her as Christ loved the Church and gave Himself for her. To refuse to do so, to have ill-will (malevolence) toward her, to see her as an object and a servant for my glory, is NOT living with her.

Abuse is, therefore, desertion. It is grounds for divorce. (27)

Adultery is often thought to just be illicit sex. However, the Jewish Talmud and Midrash also warn against "adultery" in reference to inappropriate thoughts and heart desire. It may have nothing to do with physical sex. Today, we refer to this as an emotional affair, and studies prove that emotional adultery, just as emotional abuse, is actually more hurtful and harmful than the physical act of sex or abuse.

Jesus, in his Sermon on the Mount, refers to emotional adultery when he says, "But I say to you that everyone who looks at a woman with lust has already committed adultery with her in his heart." (Matthew 5:28). Thus, Jesus indicates the heart has already engaged in adultery - nothing there about it being strictly sexual!

Emotional affairs result in feelings of being lied to, deceived and betrayed - feelings similar to your spouse having an illicit affair. The key to determining whether emotional or physical behavior can be classified as an affair is whether or not it is cloaked in SECRECY.

Because a person's limited time, energy and affection are saved now for someone other than their spouse, it is very easy for emotional abuse to be used against the innocent spouse as a way to help ease the guilt of what is going on secretly. No good thing can ever come of it, and the damage cannot always be repaired. Victims of spousal affairs often say the worst part of the affair was not the act itself, but the deception.

Like any sin, emotional affairs don't stay just emotional. They start with a friendship commonly developed at work, church or through social media. Without safeguards in place and a healthy marriage, the friendship begins to meet the need for attention, affection and approval. If allowed to continue, it will eventually escalate into a full-blown sexual affair. Sex is just a natural procession of what is already active adultery, unfaithfulness and infidelity.

Besides adultery and abandonment, there are other heart issues that your husband may have that may be contributing to the breach of covenant in your marriage. Where adultery or abandonment are, there is usually some version of these next six apertures from marital unity.

3. Lust

Lust refers to "earnest desire." Again, it is a matter of the heart as Jesus pointed out. For example, if your husband longs for the non-sexual companionship or comfort of another woman, it may still be regarded as adultery.

Your husband promised when he married you to be faithful to YOU. You expected his heart's desire would remain for you. When his heart strays, and his thoughts are continually with someone else, he is committing adultery. He may never touch her, and she may be totally unaware of his desire for her. But God knows. You probably suspect it, too.

Those who "earnestly desire" (the actual meaning of the Greek word we often translate as lust) another woman (for whatever reason), who have "set their heart upon" one other than their covenant spouse, are guilty of an inner breach of their covenant vows. (Matthew 5:27-28)

This includes pornography. I definitely considered my husband's viewing of porn to be adulterous. His lust for alcohol and drugs was a losing battle too. Those always came first before the family. In both of these examples, my husband's thoughts and desires were for something or someone other than me. At first I tried to compete with both the porn and the alcohol/drugs, but soon realized that I could not. They would always come before me and be accompanied by lies, deception, risk of disease, risk of death and violence. His desire was bound to them, not me. He foolishly thought he could have a divided heart and I should not be bothered by it. Realizing I was not a treasured part of his life was a crushing and devastating breach of covenant.

4. Idolatry

Greek scholar W. E. Vine informs us that the Greek word *moicheia* has a broader sense than the sexual. Vine points out that the concept of adultery is "breach of relationship." This covers any action and attitude that contributes to that breach of covenant. For example, he wrote,

> ... in Israel the breach of their relationship with God through their idolatry, was described as "adultery" or "harlotry"... so believers who cultivate friendship with the world, thus breaking their spiritual union with Christ, are spiritual "adulteresses" having been spiritually united to Him as wife to husband... It is used adjectively to describe the Jewish people in transferring their affections from God. (28)

Consider, too, that idolatry and mental adultery combine in viewing pornography. A centerfold is a two-dimensional, lithographic "image" before which the lecherous worshiper bows in devotion.

Matthew 12:39 and 16:4, as well as Mark 8:38, speak of a "wicked and adulterous generation." They were condemned for their lack of faith, their disobedience and their sense of shame for the Lord and his teachings. This may have had nothing to do with sex. When we turn from God to the world, we break covenant with him, and we are characterized as a "wicked and adulterous generation."

Adultery is unfaithfulness in any form. The Bible links the concept of "adultery" with faithlessness to a covenant relationship with God, which may be brought about by any number of things, chief of which seemed to be idolatry.

In summary, the "essence of adultery" is unfaithfulness in a covenant relationship, which manifests itself in any number of ways. The outcome is the breakdown of the relationship, the violation of a covenant.

5. Physical and Sexual Abuse

Physical and sexual abuse of children or yourself constitute a complete and total breach of one's marital obligations and do not require you to stay bound to your spouse. It is based on the tragedy that many men violate God's design for marriage in the darkest, most destructive terms.

Paul describes marriage in terms of God's highest design. Husbands are to love their wives as Christ loved the church and gave himself up for her. Ephesians 5:25-33 must be studied and taken seriously as to what the love of a husband looks like in a marriage. Love, in this passage, can be defined as a husband acting selflessly to meet the legitimate needs of his wife.

There is absolutely no way our loving Father condemns you for leaving physical and/or sexual abuse and getting a divorce. You need to protect children in particular if they are suffering sexual abuse, or are at risk of it. Get out, and do it with God's full blessing and help. God does NOT require you to stay in that destructive, violent situation. The entire Bible condemns this abuse because it completely goes against God's nature and character. Reread the first section on abandonment. If physical and sexual abuse is taking place, there is no question that your husband has already abandoned you and the children. He has already broken the covenant. You are released.

6. Fraud

You married your husband believing that there had been full disclosure. You find out later that he withheld information that would have adversely affected your decision to marry him. A "suppression of truth" quickly becomes a "misrepresentation" which often has legal consequences. His intention must be to gain an advantage over you by withholding information. This is a faulty contract to begin with and God will not hold you to it.

While Brian's testimony included a general confession of a criminal life lived before Christ, he left out some significant information that I would never have accepted for marriage, even with such an impressive testimony. Of course, he knew this and withheld it from me. This is fraud.

7. Fear for Your Life

You may have actually experienced an attempt on your life, or what you may consider a credible threatening of your life. For example, I became increasingly alarmed as, toward the end of our relationship, Brian repeatedly talked to me about how in prison he had learned how to kill someone and get away with it. He enjoyed describing the various methods to me. Since he knew that I was increasingly unhappy with our marriage, I felt he was giving me a cloaked warning of what would happen to me if I tried to leave him. I began to live in constant fear of dying from an "accident" or by "natural means" by his hands.

Dr. Robi Ludwig, author of *Till Death Do Us Part: Love, Marriage and the Mind of the Killer Spouse*, lists some traits of a potential spouse killer:

- Intense controlling behavior
- Explosive feelings of rage
- Difficulty forming intimate relationships
- Poor impulse control
- Inability to understand your feelings
- Absence of emotions like remorse and sympathy
- Searches out easy pleasure (i.e. a thrill seeker)
- Intense feelings of victimization and rejection
- Devalues human life
- Pathologically idealizes partner (29)

The National Center on Domestic and Sexual Violence has a revealing report on *Predictors of Domestic Violence Homicide*. It says that "the strongest contextual risk factor for intimate partner homicide is an abuser's lack of employment" increasing the risk fourfold. The less education an abuser has increases his violence also. Other factors listed as predictive of femicide are: access to firearms, use of illicit drugs, living with the abuser prior to marriage, separating, having a child who is not the abuser's biological child, threats with a weapon, and threats to kill. (Note: other experts say that threats to kill can be made subtly or directly - both are significant predictors of violence.)

They also say that an abuser's previous arrest of domestic violence actually *decreases* the risk for femicide. Arrest can be protective against domestic violence escalating to lethality. (30)

8. Passive Neglect

Pastor Jeff Crippen addresses the issue of men who are not violent, but rather quite passive and neglectful of their wife and family:

> …There are some [men] who simply are passive. They are the sluggard of Proverbs 6:9-11, "(9) How long will you lie there, O sluggard? When will you arise from your sleep? (10) A little sleep, a little slumber, a little folding of the hands to rest, (11) and poverty will come upon you like a robber, and want like an armed man."
>
> Is this abuse? What is the wife of such a man to do? We hold that an abuse victim is biblically justified in divorcing the abuser who torments her as he seeks power and control over her. But, what about this kind of passive neglect?
>
> Well, once again I think it helps for us to remind ourselves that marriage is a covenant. Scripture says so (Proverbs 2:16-17; Ezekiel 16:8; Malachi 2:14). And covenants have terms. Stipulations. They are made in the presence of God and witnesses, asking God to bless us for keeping the vows and to curse us if we break them. Pretty serious stuff…
>
> The sluggard, in his passivity, is actively violating those sacred vows. Over time, as he persists in unrepentant sluggardly, not loving his wife who is his own flesh, he destroys the covenant. Is this abuse? Well, call it what you will, it certainly is unfaithfulness to the vow-terms of the covenant, and for that reason I maintain it is indeed grounds for divorce. The wife is not required to divorce him, but I believe a case could be made that she should separate from him and that her church should assist her in doing so. Why? Well, listen to this -
>
> 2 Thessalonians 3:10-15, "(10) For even when we were with you, we would give you this command: If anyone is not willing to work, let him not eat. (11) For we hear that some among you walk in idleness, not busy at work, but busybodies. (12) Now such persons we command and encourage in the Lord

Jesus Christ to do their work quietly and to earn their own living. (13) As for you, brothers, do not grow weary in doing good. (14) If anyone does not obey what we say in this letter, take note of that person, and have nothing to do with him, that he may be ashamed. (15) Do not regard him as an enemy, but warn him as a brother."

We are not proposing here some kind of checklist procedure that is to be applied in every case like this, but surely we can see here that the Lord tells us how to deal with a man who passively abuses his family by not working, by not providing for them. (Incidentally, by "provide for them," we simply mean that he do so to the best of his ability). The church is to take this thing very seriously. Such a man, who professes to be a Christian, is living in a worse manner than an unbeliever! It is a shame to the name of Christ. We are to take note of him and have nothing to do with him. We are to warn him, and pray that this process so shame him that he will repent. (31)

As I hope you can see, divorce is a biblical concession in our imperfect world for unfaithfulness in marriage. God knew that in some marriages, sin would create unbearable circumstances, and there would need to be a way of escape for victims. <u>The covenant is breached by the person choosing not to fulfill his or her part of the covenant</u>. Divorce is merely a public and legal recognition of that breach. Blaming the victim for someone else's sin is wrong.

Idolizing the institution of marriage above the lives bound up in it is just that - idolatry and misplaced zeal. In God's love and compassion, he has provided a way of escape from terminally ill and destructive marriages. There is forgiveness, hope, and a future free from spiritual condemnation.

Don Francisco offers a good closing of common sense and reality in his article *Marriage and Divorce Myth 2 - Is Divorce a Sin?*:

> It is impossible for all divorces to be automatically sinful because God has been through divorce. That's right, check it out in Jeremiah 3:8 "Lo I had put her out and given her a certificate of divorce"...He is speaking of Israel.
>
> Whether you consider this a literal divorce or not, if ALL divorces were a sin, you can bet those words would never have escaped Him... Both marriage and divorce can be sinful depending on the circumstances. In an absolutely perfect world,

> the union between a man and a woman would be perfectly initiated by God and there would not be any destructive forces tearing at the bond. Marriages would never break down.
>
> But this isn't a perfect world and some marriages become so emotionally, spiritually, and/or physically destructive that divorce can be life saving. That is why it is dangerous to slap a grid of legalism onto yourself or others.
>
> The Bible does not forbid divorce, but God calls us to examine our hearts and to follow His specific leading. God wants us to live abundantly in His blessings. He will not entrap us, or force us to stay in our own traps to uphold an institution. The institutions of our loving God are never more important than the people within them…
>
> Galations states that we are no longer under law, but under grace. It is monumentally unhealthy to contend for a marriage on the basis that it is the legalistic and religiously correct thing to do… (32)

Perhaps you see that you fall within the biblical guidelines for leaving your spouse. You are not just bored with your marriage and wanting to try something new. You really are in a bad situation, there has been a serious breach of the marriage covenant, and you can see that God has made concessions for you to get out without any condemnation from him.

So let's look now at options you may be thinking about, such as separation, staying with him, counseling or divorce. We will examine how to settle the issue in a way that helps you experience God's peace and assurance with your choice.

Chapter Five

Options

1. Staying
2. Separating
3. Counseling or Mediation
4. Turning to the Church for Help
5. Divorce

Before I made my final decision to flee from Brian, I explored other options. In this chapter, I want to talk about some of the spiritual issues I grappled with in association with these options. Maybe it can help bring some clarity to your own situation. Figuring out what to do about an abusive relationship is complex, confusing and further complicated by religious beliefs. There are numerous dynamics involved, particularly if there are children. There is rarely one perfect solution and each option has its own advantages and risks. People who don't understand abuse and the accompanying impoverishment think victims should "just leave." As we know, it is not that simple and easy.

1. Staying

At first, I tried to just live with Brian's increasingly toxic behavior. I pacified him, catered to him, and pretended to him, myself, my kids, and other people that everything was great in our lives. That is what described this phase the most: agonizing pretense. Living a lie is hard work!

To create and maintain a pretension of something untrue, we must necessarily allow our authentic selves to die. We must become untrue to our own uniquely created and gifted person. This is extraordinarily painful because it completely goes against what God wants and what he created us to be. Worse, we aren't even able to reach out to others, either to receive or give help and support. Our world closes in and it's suffocating.

Everything good that we care about must slowly die as our abuser takes over our very identity. That is the price paid for staying with an unrepentant abuser. For me, staying with Brian meant I compromised, I forgave, I submitted, I gave in… I nearly gave up. He didn't do any of those things for me and our relationship. It was all me doing the giving and changing.

This is WRONG, and why understanding the true biblical definition of submission is so important. An abuser's definition of "submission" is anything but biblical! All it does is feed sin (abuse), and sin is never satisfied! It always demands more until it has sucked away every ounce of life and individuality the victim has.

June Hunt, counselor, author, and founder of the ministry *Hope For The Heart*, offers a six step strategy to counter verbal and emotional abuse if you want to stay in the relationship. Depending on the severity of abuse in your home, these suggestions may work. They did not work for me because Brian didn't see me as someone who had a right to independent thinking or acting. Any attempt at standing up for myself was met with stony angry silence at best. However, they might be helpful for you to try:

> 1: Clearly state what you are willing to accept and are not willing to accept from the abuser. Communicate your position in positive terms. Keep your statement short and succinct. Don't justify and don't apologize. Simply state your boundaries. "I want our relationship to continue, but I'm not willing to listen to name calling… I'm not willing to hear your accusations… I'm not willing to endure any longer the onslaught of profanity."
>
> 2: Announce the consequence you will enforce if the abuser violates your boundary. Consequences are part of God's divine plan that what we sow, we will reap. Galatians 6:7 (NIV) states, "A man reaps what he sows." Repercussions should include disengaging or distancing yourself from the abuser. You can't change the abuser, but you can remove yourself from frequent exposure to unacceptable behavior. "I want to be with you, but if you call me any kind of name again, I will leave for a time… If you persist in making that accusation, I will end our conversation… If you choose to use profanity, I will choose to be with others where we can share positive, healthy conversations."

3: Enforce the consequence every single time the abuse occurs. Do not bluff! The abuser needs to know that you will follow through consistently. Plan on being tested multiple times. In your mind and heart, say no to manipulation, no to pressure, no to control. Eventually, there's a good chance your abuser will stop... but only after the behavior proves to be ineffective. James 5:12 (ESV) says, "...let your 'yes' be yes and your 'no' be no."

4: Absolutely do not negotiate. Since abusers do not use words fairly, negotiation will not work. Instead of "talking out" the problem, your abuser will seek to wear you out! Therefore, state that when the negative behavior stops, you look forward to a renewed relationship. "I am not willing to discuss this topic further... I've stated clearly what I will not accept... When you're ready to respect my requests, let me know. I look forward to being together at that time." Keep your words brief and to the point. Proverbs 10:19 (NIV) warns that, "Sin is not ended by multiplying words, but the prudent hold their tongues."

5: Never "react" when your boundary is violated... only respond. Expect your boundary to be violated again and again! If you react, you will find yourself back under the abuser's control. Respond by detaching yourself from the abuser and enforcing your repercussions. Expect your abuser to use manipulative maneuvers. Don't cry. Don't beg. Don't explode. Expect your abuser to have emotional ups and downs. Expect your abuser to be angry with the boundary you have set. But don't seek to placate - it won't work. Take to heart Ecclesiastes 7:8-9 (NIV): "The end of a matter is better than its beginning, and patience is better than pride. Do not be quickly provoked in your spirit, for anger resides in the lap of fools."

6: Solicit the support of one or two wise, objective people to help you through this process. Include supporters as you analyze the problem, formulate your plan and enforce the repercussions. Trusted individuals - friends, mentors, counselors - can help you through this critical period. Discuss the situation with your supporters, including tactics used on you. Proverbs 19:20 (NIV) says, "Listen to advice and accept discipline, and at the end you will be counted among the wise." (33)

If you do stay, what are the ramifications to your children?

Domestic abuse and violence doesn't only affect you. You may think, as I did, that if there is no actual physical violence then kids aren't affected, but they are. They are keen observers and they are learning about relationships from the example set before them. Growing up in a dysfunctional home sets them up to repeat the cycle of abuse in their own relationships because they think it is normal. Children's tender spirits are sensitive to the stressful unhappy atmosphere of the home.

According to Alison Cunningham & Linda Baker at the *Centre for Children and Families in the Justice System*, there are 10 effects on a child in an abusive home:

- Children are denied a good father and positive male role model.
- Abuse can harm the mother/child bond.
- Children can develop negative core beliefs about themselves.
- Children can become isolated from helpful sources of support.
- Unhealthy family roles can evolve in homes with domestic violence.
- Abuse destroys a child's view of the world as a safe and predictable place.
- Abuse co-occurs with other stresses and adversities with negative effects.
- A child's style of coping and survival may become problematic.
- Children may adopt some of the rationalizations for abuse.
- Children can believe that victimization is inevitable or normal.(34)

Cunningham and Baker also explain the effects of coercive control tactics on a mother, though I will just list them briefly here. The source for this is a free PDF that is excellent for explaining the effects of abuse on mothers and their children and I would encourage you to read it in full.

- Woman believes she is an inadequate parent
- Woman loses the respect of some or all children

- Woman believes man's excuses for abuse and reinforces them with children
- Woman changes her parenting style in response to abuser's parenting style
- Woman's capacity to manage is thwarted or overwhelmed
- Woman may use survival strategies with negative effects
- Woman's bond to children is compromised
- Woman gets trapped in competition for children's loyalties (34)

Lindsey Holcomb and Justin Holcomb expound at length on the effects of domestic violence on children in their book *Is It My Fault: Hope and Healing for Those Suffering Domestic Violence*. In summary, they say:

> To begin with, studies suggest that between 10-15 million children are exposed to domestic violence every year. And for these children, abusive adults can cause tremendous long-term physical, emotional, and spiritual damage in their lives. This is true even if they [the abusers] physically abuse the mother (but the children are not physically hurt), though roughly half of men who physically abuse their wives also abuse their children. Bruce Perry, one of the top neurological trauma researchers in the world, has conclusively shown that when young children merely witness domestic violence, this trauma exposure creates long-term physiological changes, including significant structural alteration and damage to the brain.

> Lindsey and Justin go on to describe the "aftermath of abuse" in children: higher suicide attempts, drug and alcohol abuse, running away, prostitution, committing sexual assault crimes, emotional and behavioral disturbances, feelings of powerlessness and humiliation, loss of innocence and feeling safe, anxiety and fear, self-blame, shame, responsibility, guilt and anger. They continue:

> And here, among children, we see one of the most toxic effects of the cycle of abuse: Witnessing violence from one parent or caregiver to another is the strongest risk factor of transmitting violent behavior from one generation to the next. Boys who witness domestic violence are twice as likely to abuse their own partners and children when they become adults... girls who

> grow up in physically abusive homes are more likely to be physically and sexually victimized by their own intimate partners in adulthood... Children who've grown up in abusive households are 15 times more likely to be abused by other adults.
>
> If you are reading this and are still on the fence about getting out of the relationship... studies point to destructive effects of abuse that are long-term. Even if your child has not personally suffered abuse yet, the consequences of even witnessing it in the home over the rest of their lives could be catastrophic. (35)

As if this isn't enough, another issue we as mothers must grapple with is, What if I leave and he gets custody of the children? Then I won't be there to protect them. At least now, I am in the home and able to care for them.

That is a completely valid concern and one that has no easy answer. However, just being aware that your children are being negatively affected gives you power to counter the effects as best you can. Instead of just blindly hoping for the best, you can be proactive in protecting and helping them. In addition, Appendix A has applicable Bible verses you can pray over yourself and your children during this difficult time of life.

<u>How are you affected?</u>

Staying with an abuser is spiritually risky. Has your husband's sin become malignant to your faith? Are you weakening spiritually and starting to stray from your marriage vows? Are you starting to look at porn with him, drink and drug to please him or soothe your own pain? Are you finding yourself drawn to the comfort and attention of another man?

Your husband's sin is not license for you to sin. This will only cause more problems, guilt and regret. Furthermore, any questionable behavior you engage in now will be used against you down the road as 1. A personal unforgivable judgment against your character and 2. Your husband will use it against you legally. People who are ignorant about the dynamics of abuse will grab hold of any little straw and use it to build a monumental case against you, your character, and your competence.

Since most abusers are charming, persuasive and unhampered by conscience, they will relish swaying EVERYONE'S opinion against mean selfish you, and for poor innocent him. Unfair? Yes it certainly is. That is the reality. That doesn't mean you can't overcome it. It's just going to be a battle and the less you have to explain later on, the better.

<u>Another reason you may have for staying is that you think God is punishing you for being a bad Christian, or for past mistakes.</u>

I hope that chapter three helped to resolve this issue by showing how much God loves you and does not punish you for the past. We all make bad choices and end up in bad situations at times. God is not punishing you for that. Making occasional mistakes is not remotely close to being habitually controlling and abusive. This book is about unrepentant and deliberate abuse, as I defined in chapter one.

Reverend Marie Fortune says in her book *Keeping the Faith: Guidance for Christian Women Facing Abuse*:

> There may be things in your past that you regret having done or that you are not particularly proud of. There may be sins of which you have not repented. You may not go to church regularly or do all the things that you think make a good Christian. But no matter what kinds of things you have done or neglected to do, you do not deserve to be abused, and God does not send this abuse to you as punishment. If there are things that you carry that you want to repent of, then talk to God about those things in prayer. But do not excuse your husband's abusive behavior by deciding that it is God's will for you. The battering is not God's fault; it is the responsibility of your husband. He has chosen to treat you this way; it is not God's will for you. (36)

God does not want you ensnared in things that damage you spiritually, emotionally, mentally, or physically. Your husband is NOT worth losing your peace, your faith, or your integrity over. He is not worth your children growing up emotionally and spiritually bankrupt.

The consequences of staying in an atmosphere of sin and rebellion can have devastating effects on you and your children. There is a difference between staying out of guilt and fear, and staying with a plan in place and peace in your heart. Chapter seven will deal with the paralyzing giant of fear so that you can make decisions with peace and assurance.

You and your children are infinitely precious to God! That's why God has made separation and divorce a concession in grace on behalf of you, the innocent party, so that you can leave the destructive environment and be safe. God not only offers divorce as a concession, but promises to walk with you through every phase of your relationship. He is not going to abandon you.

2. Separating

If you think you are trapped with no way out, but are not ready to pursue a divorce, consider an informal or legal separation. This can provide some time and distance to cool off and decide if you feel the relationship is redeemable or not. Of course, your husband has to be okay with this. Brian wouldn't let me do this no matter how reasonable my arguments for it were. But perhaps it is an option in your case.

If your husband claims he is going to change, then separation can be a good time for you to do some self-care, reflection and healing. A *Batterer's Intervention Program* for him and counseling for you, along with additional support from others can make a world of difference in reducing the confusion and imbalance you feel.

I strongly recommend attending domestic violence support groups at your local women's shelter, crisis center or church. The knowledge you will gain from it, and the friendships you will make with others experiencing the same thing you are, will be life changing. It will also take time to see how committed he is to changing.

I asked Brian for a temporary separation, but was denied. He wouldn't even comment on my requests. For him there was no issue that needed resolved, except for me to shut up and be happy with what I had. Occasionally he would tell me, "You will never find anyone as good to you as I am. You should be grateful you have it so good."

Nonetheless, I cautiously asked about three times, offered practical solutions to any obstacles, and promoted the positive things it could do for our relationship. At that time, I was still under the illusion that our problems could be fixed if I just tried harder. I saw it as an "us" or "me" problem. I didn't yet see it as a "he is a batterer I cannot fix" problem.

After he won me over into marriage, Brian did not show respect for me, or interest in my needs or ideas. He certainly didn't believe that I would ever have the guts to leave since I was a full time mother and financially dependent on him. He refused to acknowledge that there was any problem between us, and if there was no problem then there was nothing to fix. My grief and heartache was always met with stony silence and then perhaps a demeaning change of subject as if I had never said anything. Or he would demand sex.

I finally realized that I had to make a choice. I either stayed, knowing that the girls and I were in harm's way, or I had to literally flee to get us out. I knew Brian would never let us just walk away. I made a strategic plan of escape with some trusted people, and followed through. After we left, Brian waffled between phony remorse and venomous threats if we did not return.

However, just a short time away from him helped me to think more clearly and see him for the controlling manipulative abuser he really was. Trying to see it when I was with him was like looking at him through a dense fog. Distance from him brought clarity and perspective, and allowed me to talk to other people without fear of reprisal. I never did return home, and he showed himself over the following year to not love or care about the girls or I.

The emotional and psychological hell of trying to permanently detach from Brian and keep the girls safe was worse than when we had lived with him. But God... I could never have done it without him upholding me every day. He brought us through and opened my eyes to see that what I had originally thought would just be a temporary separation from Brian needed to be permanent. The resulting hardship was worth it to be able to have the lives of peace, freedom and joy that we now enjoy.

Every situation is going to be different. Don't be afraid to do what you have to do to protect yourself and your children. It's going to be hard, but it will end eventually. The time after I left Brian was definitely harder than the time I was with him. Leaving an abuser, even temporarily, is no cakewalk.

But you can do it and come out the other side so much better off. Things won't always go the way you want them to. That's why prayer, listening to your instincts, and receiving WISE counsel and support from others is so important. We all need each other - this is a battle you aren't meant to figure out and fight alone.

Remember that the risk of lethality goes way up when you leave an abuser. It's the most dangerous time period, so I strongly recommend surrounding yourself with a support system from your local women and children's shelter before you do leave. Even if you think he won't do anything - leaving even for just a little while can trigger some pretty nasty responses that you don't expect. He really believes you and the children are his property. Protect yourself and be smart, but don't stay just because of the risk. Appendix C has a risk assessment you can take right now, and Appendix D has a good safety plan.

3. Counseling or Mediation

Counseling should be individual, NOT couples counseling. In an abusive marriage, couples counseling is inappropriate and will frequently make the abuse worse.

I also strongly advise against turning to your pastor for counseling, unless you know that he has been trained in the dynamics of domestic abuse and violence. Otherwise, you will likely be sent back to your husband and your situation will worsen. Appropriate clergy involvement is explained in the next section.

Pastor Jeff Crippen advises those considering counseling or mediation:

> When we are dealing with an abusive person, the solution is not to just "sit down and talk, work things out, communicate and understand one another better." NO! Because as we have been learning, the abusive man or woman has no intent at all to work things out. He or she knows nothing of compromising, of empathizing, of kindness. He only knows power and control and entitlement. Therefore, any such meeting with an abuser will only result in giving the abusive man another opportunity to abuse his victim.
>
> This is a vital lesson to learn then in respect to dealing with an abusive person. Such a person… has only one purpose - to destroy, to discourage, to instill fear, to mock and rob his victim of any sense of self-worth and confidence… to control, to own, to exercise power, to be as God to his victims. Therefore, it is not wise to enter into mediation with an abuser. It is not wise to enter into couples' counseling with an abuser.
>
> Communication problems are NOT the problem. The abusive person's mentality is the problem, and it is his problem alone… Like Nehemiah in his dealings with Sanballat [Nehemiah 6:1-13], the Christian is NOT bound to meet with an abusive person. We are NOT obligated to maintain an abusive relationship, thereby permitting the abuser to continue in his power and control and abuse…

Mediation, communication, reconciliation and peace-making requires goodwill from both parties. But as we have seen, the abuser has no goodwill - he is malevolent toward his victims. He will only use such sessions to exercise more of his abuse, to work more of his deceptions, and to make it appear to the foolish that he is the one who truly wants to set things right. (37)

4. Turning to the Church for Help

This is a topic I feel very strongly about. I have, more often than not, witnessed the devastating effects of clergy discounting a victim's disclosure of abuse. When men of the cloth minimize us as abuse victims, it carries an extra load of pain because we trust them and their representation of God's values. Christian leaders are supposed to live by a higher standard, yet often they carelessly act in ways that are an affront to the nature of God.

That said, there are religious clergy, leaders and influencers who do "get it" about domestic violence and they are speaking out boldly about it. There is an increase in domestic violence trainings in churches and a growing awareness that the church has long dropped the ball on this vital topic. I include links to many of these people in the resources section and encourage you to visit their websites for in-depth help.

I personally do NOT recommend turning to the church first, if at all, for help.

The feelings of shock, betrayal, disappointment, and probable shunning hits victims hard, especially when they are at their weakest. They assume that the leadership at their church will understand their plight and have compassion and good counsel. They assume church is a safe place for them. Instead, leadership will usually blame the victim and justify the abuser. Even more so if the abuser has an important position in the church. It's incredibly painful to experience on top of everything else going on.

Of course, if you are blessed enough to be part of a church that understands the truth about domestic violence and responds appropriately, then by all means utilize their support and be thankful for such a blessing! Let other victims know it is a safe church for them.

Reverend Marie Fortune expresses well the reality of religious betrayal:

> If you have not yet talked with your pastor or priest about the abuse you have experienced, there is probably a good reason. You probably intuitively sense that he or she will not be helpful to you. This may be because you have never heard your clergy person mention anything about wife abuse. Or it may be because you have heard something mentioned that made it clear that your experience would not be understood or believed. Trust your feelings about this. Do not go to this person unless you feel safe and assured that your clergyperson will listen, understand, and believe you. If you are simply unsure, take someone with you - preferably a shelter counselor or support group leader who can support you and help your pastor or priest learn about your situation. (38)

Carolyn Heggen, author of *Sexual Abuse in Christian Homes and Churches* says:

> The church, past and present, has accepted and promoted a patriarchal agenda. In its teaching, practice, exegesis, and preaching, the church has perpetuated an ideology about men, women, and children in general - and about sexuality and abuse in particular - which has sustained the very foundation of the widespread problem of sexual violence… For every minister who says, "But no one ever comes to me with this problem!" there are dozens of victims, survivors, and perpetrators who desperately need the ministry of the church.

> Whether through passive denial or active efforts to silence victims and survivors, the church contradicts its own mandate to justice… In fact, Scripture mandates the church to stand with those who are objects of harm and exploitation, to protect the little ones, to offer hospitality to the vulnerable, to set free those imprisoned by social convention. Jesus' ministry with women and children provides an unequivocal model of justice-making as the appropriate response to the injustices heaped on the oppressed. (39)

What a typical church response looks like.

Pastor Jeff Crippen lays out a typical church response to abuse scenario in his book *A Cry for Justice: How the Evil of Domestic Abuse Hides in Your Church*. In my experience also, this is normally how it plays out. It really doesn't vary much, and neither does the ending devastation. Consider this scenario carefully before you turn to your church. If you have already experienced this, then just knowing you are not alone may be of some comfort.

1. Victim reports abuse to her pastor.

2. Pastor does not believe her claims, or at least believes they are greatly exaggerated. After all, he "knows" her husband to be one of the finest Christian men he knows, a pillar of the church.

3. Pastor minimizes the severity of the abuse. His goal is often, frankly, damage control (to himself and to his church).

4. Pastor indirectly (or not so indirectly!) implies that the victim needs to do better in her role as wife and mother and as a Christian. He concludes that all such scenarios are a "50/50" blame sharing.

5. Pastor sends the victim home, back to the abuser, after praying with her and entrusting the problem to the Lord.

6. Pastor believes he has done his job.

7. Victim returns, reporting that nothing has changed. She has tried harder and prayed, but the abuse has continued.

8. Pastor decides to do some counseling...

9. As time passes, the victim becomes the guilty party in the eyes of the pastor and others. She is the one causing the commotion. She is pressured by the pastor and others in the church to stop rebelling, to submit to her husband, and stop causing division in the church.

10. After more time passes, the victim separates from or divorces the abuser. The church has refused to believe her, has persistently covered up the abuse, has failed to obey the law and report the abuse to the police, and has refused to exercise church discipline against the abuser. Ironically, warnings of impending church discipline are often directed against the victim!

> 11. The final terrible injustice is that the victim is the one who must leave the church, while the abuser remains a member in good standing, having successfully duped the pastor and church into believing that his victim was the real problem. (40)

I see this scenario repeatedly played out in the lives of women I serve, not only for laywomen in the congregation, but also for wives of abusive church leaders and pastors. It is also common that when the wife leaves the church and starts attending another, the abuser will follow her and turn the new church against her. He will do this repeatedly, making it impossible for her to attend any church in peace. The church believes her abuser's claims right away and frowns at her for causing problems and making life difficult for everyone else. They pity the abuser for having to live with such a selfish troublemaker. She is stigmatized wherever she goes.

Catherine Clark Kroeger, President Emerita, Christians for Biblical Equality:

> Domestic violence ranks as the number one public health problem for women in America, and yet those of the cloth prefer to look the other way. They know, of course, that incidents do happen, but not in their congregation. Their folk are too nice, too spiritual, too well taught, too well balanced, too mature, too upstanding, and too discreet. A prime defense is to deny that the problem exists, even though the evidence tells us that there is a strong likelihood of spousal abuse in every faith community.
>
> If an admission must be made, pastors often minimize, conceal, or ignore the reality. Few dare to speak directly to the perpetrator about the problem. Many prefer to dodge so embarrassing and uncomfortable an issue. The truth is that they simply do not know what to do in abusive family situation. Many clergy persons have followed popular evangelical trends in idolizing and idealizing the family.
>
> The bible, however, speaks forthrightly of troubled families and of God's redemptive work among them. Honesty, not silence, is the key to healing… Although victims turn more often to their pastors than to all other resources combined, clergy

and other pastoral ministers simply have not been equipped to meet the challenge. (41)

<u>What happens when the church sides with the abuser.</u>

Religious leaders are usually esteemed in our society. When they respond to a disclosure of abuse with compassion and knowledge of the dynamics, it can be healing and lifesaving to the victim and her children. However, when they side with patriarchal tradition, they not only re-victimize the wife, but they add spiritual abuse on top of the domestic abuse she is already burdened under.

Leaders may also feel they can take a neutral stance between the husband and wife. However, neutrality really means siding with the abuser, because they are effectively saying that it is not abuse. Either way, the abuser is enabled to continue and actually accelerate the abuse.

Pastor Jeff Crippen:

> Christian" support/enabling of the abuser makes him conclude that God is on his side. That he is in the right. It makes him out to be a holy jihadist, zealous for the Lord, ready and willing to wipe out any opposition. Christians who enable abusers actually hand over the keys to a new and improved torture chamber to the evil man, and they do so in the name of the Lord! That is blasphemy. It is using the Lord's name in vain.
>
> "… they have spoken in my name lying words that I did not command them. I am the one who knows, and I am witness, declares the LORD." (Jeremiah 29:23b)
>
> What does this say about the culpability of Christians who enable the abuser? It says that they share in the guilt for this wickedness. They participate in the oppression of the victim. They have blood on their hands.
>
> You see, while we are errant human beings, falling quite short of perfection, nevertheless there are some things we simply must get right… So, Christian, remember this and mark it down well. The next time you preach things like "just go back to him and submit and pray for him more" to victims, the next time you preach a sermon about how husbands are to be masters and priests in their home and how wives are to submit to them in all things, you are a participant in the abuse being

dished out to the victim and in fact you are increasing its severity because you have endorsed the wicked man's thinking that he has God on his side.

God is most certainly not on the abuser's side, and furthermore, He is not on yours [errant clergy] either. (42)

Proper clergy response to victims and abusers.

Dr. Russell Moore, a minister and author, gives clear instruction on how churches should respond to abusers:

> Church discipline against wife-beaters must be clear and consistent. We must stand with women against predatory men in all areas of abandonment, divorce, and neglect. We must train up men, through godly mentoring as well as through biblical instruction, who will know that the model of a husband is a man who crucifies his selfish materialism, his libidinal fantasies, and his wrathful temper tantrums in order to care lovingly for a wife. We must also remind these young men that every idle word, and every hateful act, will be laid out in judgment before the eyes of the One to whom we must give an answer. (43)

Carol Adams, author of *When the Abuser Is Among Us: One Church's Response to a Perpetrator*, has this to say about a proper response by the church to disclosure of abuse:

> Accountability or collusion. I explained that in responding to the abuser it was essential to focus on behavior, not characteristics; otherwise we may succumb to the great temptation of identifying with the perpetrator and the perpetrator's pain instead of being focused on the victim's pain. Identification with him can mean that we feel anxiety over his being called to accountability and may prevent us from doing what he most needs. Within Christian communities there is often confusion about calling to accountability in that we think that being loving and Christ like is releasing someone from their sufferings, rather than saying, "I will be with you as you experience the consequences of your behavior." (44)

Pastor Jeff Crippen lays out some practical guidelines to keep in mind if you are going to say anything to your church. Compare their response to what Pastor Jeff lays out as a proper response to you:

- Clergy will believe you. This is not blind acceptance but a knowledge that "in most cases those who report abuse are speaking with honesty."
- They will not be influenced based on who the abuser is, understanding that all forms of abuse (not just physical or sexual) are serious.
- They will report abuse to police and allow the justice system to act.
- They will protect you from accusations.
- They will dissuade you from attempting to cover up the abuse.
- They will preach on the topic of abuse to prepare and protect the congregation.
- As clergy deals with the abuser, they will:
- Question everything. Even "facts" he states with absolute confidence.
- Believe nothing without corroboration.
- Assume he is attempting to deceive them.
- Accept nothing less than full, unqualified repentance.
- Will not pity him, no matter how emotional he might be.
- Accept no excuses.
- Will not let him blame others. (45)

I hope this helps you as much as it helped me. The most important thing is to not take on the inevitable feelings of anger and bitterness you will feel if your church turns against you. Know with certainty that God is angry when people wound the afflicted in his name. They are not accurately representing God at all. God is for you and is going to stand by you. Please do not turn away from him because of the foolishness, selfishness and ignorance of people who claim to be representing him. God will deal with them in his timing and wisdom. Instead, turn to God even more for comfort and a greater outpouring of his love and compassion in your life.

<u>Speaking to leadership about red flags you see in your church.</u>

This is something that comes up often with victims of abuse I talk to, and I just want to touch on it before leaving this subject of the church. When you have experienced abuse, it is easy to spot the signs of abuse elsewhere. If you are in a toxic church, you may see red flags of inappropriate behavior.

If you respectfully question (not accusing) something you see going on that you are uncomfortable with, you will possibly be told that (a) you need counseling for even thinking of it; (b) that your experience has colored your judgment; (c) that you are the one with the problem; or (d) that you are the only one to have a problem with it.

In all likelihood, this is untrue. This is a brilliant way for toxic people to shift the attention off themselves and onto your supposed inadequacy and incompetence. Since you as a victim may have poor self-esteem, this ploy works particularly well to get you off the trail if there really is something inappropriate going on. Spiritual abuse signs are similar to domestic abuse signs. In this case, toxic leadership wants to get the attention off them and onto you. This is known as *blame-shifting* and used by all abusers.

Telling a sexual abuse victim that she is not qualified to recognize signs of sexual abuse because of her experience is like telling a firefighter he is not qualified to recognize signs of a fire because of his experience. It's absurd. BECAUSE of your experience, you are more qualified to notice red flags. If someone belittles you because you have experienced something, walk away with your head high. The question of credibility is on them, not on you. Take it as the sign it is of a toxic environment you don't need to be part of.

A proper response to your concerns would be to respectfully listen and assurance of looking into the matter further. Respect, not accusation, is the key word for both sides toward each other.

Abusers (and abusive churches) don't want you to value yourself and your experience - they want you to doubt yourself, shrink back and stay quiet. I want to validate you as a person who has gained wisdom and insight from your experience. You are not crazy or inferior.

It will take time, but as you heal, you will learn that your experience is valuable and there is no shame in what you have been through. Your voice matters. Everything you have been through is going to help someone else someday, so don't shrink back in shame. Speak up if you see something that concerns you. It may very well be life-saving for someone else. How others respond is between them and God. You can move on with your self-respect and integrity intact.

Of course, if you are witnessing abuse against children, or suspect it, don't just say something to leadership and then walk away. Turn to professionals outside of the church for advice and help. Advocates at your shelter or other professional agency can give you good feedback on what you are seeing or sensing, and give proper advice on what to do about it next.

5. Divorce

We have already established that God permits divorce in cases of malignant abuse (chapter four). Since we know that God is more interested in our heart attitude, how can we be sure we have a right attitude towards biblically permissible divorce? Does it matter if a breach of covenant is a single act? Or is it an ongoing state of sin that qualifies one to pursue divorce?

For example, say you and your husband have been growing distant toward each other due to long work hours and a new baby. He has a single illicit encounter with the secretary at work.

Biblically you have the right to leave the marriage. He breached your marriage covenant. But is this really the best thing for you to do? Does it make a difference for you if it is an intermittent or isolated incident? Or is this encounter habitual?

At the least, the affair is a one-time error in judgment that possibly could be remedied. It could be a wakeup call for you as a couple to get help and find satisfying solutions for both of you. Could you forgive it and use it as a stepping-stone to a solid marriage?

Is your husband genuinely grieved over it? In this case, ask the Lord if he wants you to attempt restoration and healing. It has happened to many women who are now grateful they didn't give up on their marriage. Seek God for that leading, since he knows your husband's heart the best.

However, if you are dealing with a true abuser, this option is probably not possible. Abuse permeates every facet of life and sexual unfaithfulness is the norm rather than the exception. More than likely, to him his infidelity is no big deal. He will feel entitled to it, and even blame you for it, if not outright flaunting it in your face. He feels no remorse and has no genuine intention to change.

However the breach of covenant has taken place, your trust has been painfully trampled on. Trust is essential to a biblical marriage.

Barbara Roberts, author of *Not Under Bondage: Biblical Divorce for Abuse, Adultery and Desertion*, places the blame for the breach of covenant squarely where it belongs, on the abuser:

The perpetration of domestic abuse effectively pushes away the other spouse and divides the marriage. The fact that many victims eventually leave abusive relationships testifies to this pushing away. Perpetrators usually protest that they want the marriage to continue, but their evil conduct conveys the exact opposite - it effectually pushes the opposite spouse away.

When applying 1 Corinthians 7:15, the key question is not "Who walked out?" but "Who caused the separation?" Would it be sensible to say that David was the sinful rebellious one when he left Saul's court? No, he left because of Saul's abuse. David left, but Saul was the cause of his leaving. If we translate the word chorizo as "separate" we see this more clearly: if the unbeliever separates, let him separate. The unbeliever is doing the separating; the believer is commanded to let it be done. This tells the believing spouse (and the church) to allow the marriage to be over, because the unbeliever has destroyed the covenant. It permits the victim of abuse to take out a legal divorce. Let there be chorizo = let there be separation = let there be legal divorce, because the word chorizo means both separation and divorce... (46)

What if the abuser is a professing Christian?

Then an effort should be made to bring him to repentance, and this should be done through accountability to others such as the police, clergy and other professionals. 1 Corinthians 7:15 applies to marriages where the spouse is an unbeliever. If a professing Christian does not demonstrate genuine repentance, then according to the Bible, he should be treated as an unbeliever. The victim is then at liberty to get a divorce.

By the time a victim has come to the place of wondering about a divorce, she usually has already done a great deal to try to save the relationship. Grace and forgiveness to restore a relationship is possible where the erring partner genuinely repents. Premeditated chronic abuse, abandonment, and abnormal behaviors are at minimum very toxic, and usually terminal to a marriage covenant.

Whether you choose to end your marriage or not, it is essential that you live your life with integrity and virtue anyway. Value and protect your relationship with the Lord above anyone and anything else. If it is coming down to morally choosing whether to please God or please your husband, God must be first. He will honor you and help you through whatever you face.

God loves you deeply, and he alone understands the depth of your heartache, fears, worries, confusion and all the obstacles you are facing. No matter where you are today, what mistakes you have made, what trials you are dealing with - you can start fresh with him. He extends to you his love, grace, and an opportunity to make a fresh start!

Don't accept criticism from anyone for your choice made between you and God. If you choose to divorce, never let anyone beat you up about it. God views divorce as final (Deuteronomy 24:1-4). God is a God of fresh starts and wants to fill you with peace, forgiveness, and love (1 Corinthians 7:15). Let God be your redeemer!

<u>I left my husband and never regretted it.</u>

I worried constantly about what the effects on the kids would be whether we stayed or whether we left. When I finally left, my daughters were 2, 4 and 5 years old so please take that into consideration with my story. I was willing to live with personal pain and trauma if it was better for the kids to remain in the home just for the sake of having a father. The few people I talked to gave strong opinions about it: stay no matter how bad it is so that you don't deprive the kids of their dad; or get away and protect the children from witnessing and experiencing abuse. Both sides had a convincing argument for what they believed.

My final choice was to leave Brian to protect the girls from what I believed would be a very dark future. To my knowledge, they had not been physically or sexually abused yet, but since all the signs were pointing to imminent violation, I chose to get out before it could take place.

I didn't leave with any intention of getting a divorce. I initially left purely out of fear for my kids, and needing to get away from the environment so I could think things through more clearly. It didn't really make sense to me how valuable an abusive father could be to them. I knew many kids had grown up without fathers and were mature happy adults with healthy interpersonal relationships because they had one healthy parent who loved them. In hindsight, I can hardly believe that I ever had difficulty making the choice to leave.

But unfortunately, when a victim is in the abusive environment, nothing makes clear sense. Everything is muddled and confusing.

That's why getting away from the environment and influence of the abuser can make a world of difference in gaining clarity. Add to that gaining some insight from outsiders, particularly advocates trained in recognizing the signs of abuse, and you can really start to make progress in understanding what is happening and how you need to respond.

My decision to leave was the right one. To my surprise, all three of my daughters thanked me for getting them away from daddy and made me promise they would never have to go back to him. One of my daughters actually prayed this prayer within a week of us leaving Brian: "Dear God, thank you for getting us away from daddy. I want you to live in my heart forever because now I know that you really love us because you got us away from daddy."

That prayer came from a child who I thought was unaware of what was going on since there was no physical violence against us. My daughters never looked back after we left. They jumped into their new life full-speed with joy and energy. They developed friendships with wonderful people and began to heal, grow and thrive. My girls love the Lord, love school, have healthy relationships and support, and are growing in their unique gifts.

I share this to encourage you that kids know a lot more about what is going on than we think they do, and if we as mothers provide them with safety, security and a ton of love, they can flourish without living all the time with an abusive parent. Kids are naturally resilient, and we can nurture their resiliency by listening to them and giving them a safe environment to grow up in. Exposure to abuse does put kids at risk, but we can counteract that with our unconditional love and a supportive network.

In case you are wondering, I did file for a divorce a year after leaving. Brian threatened many horrible things and I was sick over the thought of what would happen if he was allowed to be alone with the girls. But the judge recognized the danger also and ruled to protect the girls completely from him. Brian then disappeared from our lives.

Not every case turns out that well. I know that many of you reading this have already lost custody of your children to your abuser. You have my greatest compassion and prayers. I only offer my experience to show that if you think you have to stay because your kids have to have their father full-time, that that is not necessarily true. They will probably do better not being in that toxic environment, even if only for short breaks.

Whether you stay or leave, that is something only you can decide. It is never a simple decision to make and most people do not understand the difficult dynamics surrounding the issue. To leave successfully may take months of strategically planning and preparing. Or it may be something you do overnight with no preparation because you don't have a choice in it. Don't let people who don't understand your situation place guilt trips on you. Those of us who have been down this road know all too well the hardship that accompanies it, and very few outsiders comprehend it. When they say things, take what is helpful and leave the rest behind.

In the next chapter, we are going to look at what our response to abusers should be. God wants us to respond to abusers in a right way, but what does that look like? You may not even need to know because you've decided to get out and be done with it. But if you have children together or you decide to stay with him longer, you are going to have to deal with him. We will look at the issue of forgiveness and grief, and the signs of true repentance and change.

Chapter Six

A Christian Wife's Biblical Response to Abuse

1. Response to His Abuse
2. Response to People Blaming You
3. Response to His Claimed Repentance (signs it's authentic)
4. Grief
5. Forgiveness

While I endured an unhappy marriage, I often wondered how God expected me to respond beyond submission and prayer. I was sure I wasn't supposed to violate God's moral law, but felt a conflict because Brian often did.

It's actually not a conflict when we find out what God really wants. Conflict is experienced when we don't understand God's will, which he revealed in his Word. That's why it is so important to study the Bible personally, rather than just accepting what people (even husband's and clergy) claim about it.

One thing God is very clear about is that our loyalty and love must go to him first, before anyone and anything else. Matthew 22:36-40, "(36) 'Teacher, which commandment in the law is the greatest?' (37) He [Jesus] said to him, 'You shall love the Lord your God with all your heart, and with all your soul, and with all your mind.' (38) This is the greatest and first commandment. (39) And a second is like it: 'You shall love your neighbor as yourself.' (40) On these two commandments hang all the law and the prophets."

Jesus did not say, wives shall love their husbands with all their heart, soul and mind. He said we are to love him first with everything we are!

When we elevate God to his rightful place above our husband, then confusion will lose its grip on us. 1 Corinthians 14:33 says God is not a God of confusion and disorder but of peace and order. Confusion and disorder define abusive relationships, so if the source of that is not God, then we know that the enemy of our souls is the source.

God is against injustice and the abuse of power. It doesn't matter where this is taking place, whether in a country, a community, a church, a home or a marriage. Micah 6:8, "He has told you, O mortal, what is good; and what does the Lord require of you but to do justice, and to love kindness, and to walk humbly with your God?"

When we are faced with the sin of abuse, it is tempting to react with a sinful response of our own. That may be with compromise, passiveness or overt anger in any number of ways. Please remember I am speaking in general. There are certainly times when being passive is important for safety. I'm referring to an attitude toward abuse where passivity means hopeless acceptance.

Romans 12:21 says, "Do not be overcome by evil, but overcome evil with good." 1 Peter 3:9, "Do not repay evil for evil or abuse for abuse; but, on the contrary, repay with a blessing. It is for this that you were called—that you might inherit a blessing." This indicates a proactive approach toward abuse.

Other places in the Bible talk about using wisdom in our dealings such as Ephesians 5:15-17, "Be careful then how you live, not as unwise people but as wise, making the most of the time, because the days are evil. So do not be foolish, but understand what the will of the Lord is."

Jeremiah 9:24 further reveals God's heart: "but let those who boast, boast in this, that they understand and know me, that I am the Lord; I act with steadfast love, justice, and righteousness in the earth, for in these things I delight, says the Lord."

Some of the moral dilemmas I faced with Brian were things like him wanting me to take drugs with him or selling things he stole from work. If I suspected he was cheating on me, should I keep my mouth shut or confront him? If he wanted to drive the kids somewhere while he was drunk, do I say no or cave to avoid a fight and just pray for their protection? If a man wants to visit with me, giving me some desperately needed attention, is that okay since I'm not getting that from my husband? How much lying should I do for him? Where is the boundary between having a clear conscience with God and submitting to my husband for the sake of peace? The dilemmas progressed, just as all abuse progresses in intensity and methods over time.

The Bible says we cannot serve two masters: "Am I now seeking human approval, or God's approval? Or am I trying to please people? If I were still pleasing people, I would not be a servant of Christ." (Galatians 1:10)

1. Response to His Abuse

<u>When we find ourselves in an abusive relationship, God wants us to respond with love and wisdom, and stand for justice and righteousness.</u>

Not only are we to do this for ourselves, but we are to do it for others who we see being oppressed. When there is a moral conflict between our husband or God, then God's way always overrules man's.

Responding with abusive behavior or speech when we are provoked is never justified and only makes things worse. If it was justified for us as victims, then abusive behavior by perpetrators would be justified. People will provoke us in many situations and relationships throughout life. As lovers of Christ and carriers of his nature, we are to take the high road.

For those who think there is a cut and dried response in an abusive relationship, there isn't. Often victims, knowing that a violent episode is on its way, will provoke it to get it over with as a matter of self-preservation. There is absolutely no condemnation to anyone in these dangerous situations. However, once we know that God does not want us to live under these circumstances, it frees us to explore alternatives.

God will give you wisdom to know when and how to stand for truth and righteousness. He will not demand you to do something that puts you in harm's way. What matters is coming into agreement with his will and seeking him for how to live that out in your present circumstances.

<u>God wants us to protect ourselves.</u>

Along with the principle of siding with truth and righteousness, is coming under protection. This is a biblical principle and not one you need to feel is contrary to God's will for you.

Psalms 55:4-8, "(4) My heart is in anguish within me, the terrors of death have fallen upon me. (5) Fear and trembling come upon me, and horror overwhelms me. (6) And I say, "O that I had wings like a dove! I would fly away and be at rest;(7) truly, I would flee far away; I would lodge in the wilderness; (8) I would hurry to find a shelter for myself from the raging wind and tempest."

Do you ever feel like that? I remember about a month before I decided to flee from Brian with the girls. I laid face down in a muddy pasture utterly broken and done for. I longed for the comfort of death. I didn't think I could take one more second of the anguish and fear.

There are times when the wisest thing to do is to remove yourself from a dangerous situation, if not permanently, at least temporarily. Fortunately, here in the United States, there are numerous resources available for any woman who chooses this path. It can be a much-needed reprieve where she can rest in a safe environment and figure things out with supportive and caring people.

Here are some verses showing how much God loves you and wants you to be safe. Sometimes God does miraculously deliver us from harm, but often we just need to use wisdom and run from it knowing that God is with us and will help us!

Proverbs 22:3, "The clever see danger and hide; but the simple go on, and suffer for it."

Ecclesiastics 7:12, "For the protection of wisdom is like the protection of money, and the advantage of knowledge is that wisdom gives life to the one who possesses it."

Psalm 34:7, "The angel of the Lord encamps around those who fear him, and delivers them."

Psalm 32:7, "You are a hiding place for me; you preserve me from trouble; you surround me with glad cries of deliverance. Selah."

Psalm 34:17-19, "(17) When the righteous cry for help, the LORD hears, and rescues them from all their troubles. (18) The Lord is near to the brokenhearted, and saves the crushed in spirit. (19) Many are the afflictions of the righteous, but the LORD rescues them from them all."

Psalm 5:11, "But let all who take refuge in you rejoice; let them ever sing for joy. Spread your protection over them, so that those who love your name may exult in you."

Psalm 37:40, "The Lord helps them and rescues them; he rescues them from the wicked, and saves them, because they take refuge in him."

You are valued and precious in God's eyes! He does not want you to be hurt by men who do not appreciate your worth. Being married to an abusive man does not mean you have to take whatever he dishes out to you. Just as we learned earlier in chapter three, if your husband is violent toward you, HE has already broken the marriage covenant. God does not ask you to continue to submit to that evil.

1 Corinthians 3:16-17 says God considers you his temple: "(16) Do you not know that you are God's temple and that God's Spirit dwells in you? (17) If anyone destroys God's temple, God will destroy that person. For God's temple is holy, and you are that temple."

John 10:10 "The thief comes only to steal and kill and destroy. I came that they may have life, and have it abundantly."

God wants you to live an abundant life. Is there room for fear and abuse in an abundant life? Abundant life includes feeling safe, knowing you are loved and respected.

God wants us to protect our children.

Jesus treated children with love, kindness, care and protection. In no way did Jesus ever abuse a child or condone it. There is never any justification for harshness toward children. Often Proverbs 13:24 (spare the rod, spoil the child) is misused to justify abusive behavior towards kids, but that is not what God intended. Love does not hurt!

The point of this verse is to encourage discipline, as in to guide and direct using love. In the Bible, the rod was used by the shepherd to protect and guide the sheep, or to pull them out of dangerous places. It was never used to hurt them. That's why the psalmist in Psalm 23 references the rod as comforting: "your rod and your staff - they comfort me."

God expects us as moms to take our role seriously as protectors of our children. It is NEVER okay to turn a blind eye to children suffering abuse. Of all people, moms must be there to protect and nurture the children, even if we must sacrifice our own comfort to do it.

This isn't to say that our efforts to protect our children are always successful, but we have to try our best and leave what we can't control in the Lord's hands. If you feel you can't stand up for your child out of fear of the consequences by the abuser, then it's time to reconsider staying in that relationship.

I like the website, *The Mama Bear Effect*. While they primarily address the issue of child sexual abuse, their tips on deterring abuse applies for protecting children from any kind of abuse, including from family members. I am going to paraphrase their article, but visiting the website and reading the whole article is worth it:

1. Show that you are a loving and attentive parent. Be involved in your child's life! It sends an important message to your child that they are valued, and it sends a message to abusers (including fathers) that abuse of the child is not going to be accepted.

2. Trust yourself over others and speak up if something doesn't feel right. Your instincts protect you and your child from danger, so if something doesn't feel right, have the courage to say no to it. Assuming your abusive husband has your child's best interests in mind is a mistake. If your husband doesn't have the integrity to treat you right, he doesn't have the integrity to treat anyone right, least of all the most vulnerable. If he cared about the child, he would love and respect the child's mother.

3. Respect and listen to your child. If your child knows you value their feelings and opinions, they are more likely to tell you what's going on when they are being hurt.

4. Be someone who is knowledgeable about child abuse and speaks up about it.

5. Raise your child to have faith in their self-worth and right to respect, and let others know you have taught your children. (47)

An abusive spouse is also often abusing the children. If they aren't blatantly hurting them, they may be flooding the child with attention and gifts to alienate them from you. This is also abuse.

There are certainly no guarantees that trying to save your children will work, especially since the legal system sometimes hinders a mother's ability to do that. But on a spiritual level, if you will honor God by doing what you can to protect your children, God will honor your heart and your efforts and he is able to do what we as parents can't do. Pray for your children daily, love them know matter how tough it gets, and stand up for them. Trust God to do what you cannot. He cares about them even more than you do, and when we as moms come into partnership with him, good things happen. It may take time, but time and effort spent for your children is never wasted.

When we have failed in the past, we can beat ourselves up and feel that we can never make up for it. The times I feel absolutely the worst is when I am acutely aware of my shortcomings as a parent. The enemy loves to torment us with accusations in this area.

God is not accusing you though. Satan is the accuser. Whatever has happened in the past, God is willing to forgive and let you start fresh today. Start today to find ways to be supportive of your kids. That may mean leaving your abuser and taking them to a safe house while you figure things out. Safe houses have good programs for kids to help them deal with their pain. It may mean turning your abuser in for what he has perpetrated against you and your children. It can mean many things. The point is that you need to listen to your heart and make sure your children have priority over any man in your life. While they are dependent, their needs come first. And the first need a child has is for safety: physically, emotionally and spiritually.

The decision of whether to stay or leave for the sake of the children isn't always easy to make though. There are dynamics at play that only you know about, although many will judge you harshly if you feel that staying with the abuser is in your children's best interest.

Lundy Bancroft has this to say about mom's who choose to stay with their abuser:

> There's no easy answer for the abused mother. Children don't want to lose their father, they just want his abusiveness and violence to stop. If she leaves him, she also faces economic hardships that could drag her away from her children - she might have to start working full time, for example, which could be a big loss for her and her kids if that wasn't the case before. Children who are living with an abuser in their lives NEED THEIR MOTHERS.
>
> And what if leaving him would actually mean she has less time to spend with the kids? It's hard to say if that's best. And then, the abuser is going to get visitation time, so suddenly the kids will be away from her whole weekends, half the day on their birthdays, half the day on holidays including the big religious holidays, and so forth. And finally, when his visitation starts, he's suddenly getting all this time alone with them where she has no way to keep an eye on what he's doing with them. So I think there are good reasons to leave and good reasons to stay,

and we really need to respect the choices mothers make in these horrible binds. (48)

There are many supportive communities online that can help you navigate this, especially your fear of losing them if you do stand up to the abuse, or how to deal with it if you have lost custody. It's one of the toughest things you will face, but God is greater than all of it. Put him first, seek his wisdom, pray for your children daily, and surround yourself with people who can support you because they have been through it too. I have listed in the Resources some websites that offer particularly good information and support on this subject.

There are also many programs available to help mothers be independent so they are less likely to stay in unhealthy relationships. Programs may assist with childcare, education, job opportunities, parenting skills, and financial support and literacy. You can call the National Domestic Violence Hotline at 1-800-799-7233 for your local resources.

<u>Seek help from higher authorities.</u>

One of the primary environments abuse of any kind must have to flourish is secrecy. Exposing abuse to the light is the only way for both victims and abusers to get help. Ephesians 5:11 says "Take no part in the unfruitful works of darkness, but instead expose them."

The purpose of exposing abuse is made clear in James 5:19-20, "(19) My brothers and sisters, if anyone among you wanders from the truth and is brought back by another, (20) you should know that whoever brings back a sinner from wandering will save the sinner's soul from death and will cover a multitude of sins."

It is biblical to seek help from higher authorities when you are experiencing abuse. It is biblical to flee to a shelter or to talk to the police. God put the law into place to protect victims. Domestic violence is against the law, including marital rape. Police or domestic violence agencies can talk to you about the laws in your state that can protect you.

Romans 13:1-5 says: "(1) Let every person be subject to the governing authorities; for there is no authority except from God, and those authorities that exist have been instituted by God. (2) Therefore whoever resists authority resists what God has appointed, and those who resist will incur judgment. (3) For rulers are not a terror to good conduct, but to bad. Do you wish to have no fear of the authority?

Then do what is good, and you will receive its approval; (4) for it is God's servant for your good. But if you do what is wrong, you should be afraid, for the authority does not bear the sword in vain! It is the servant of God to execute wrath on the wrongdoer. (5) Therefore one must be subject, not only because of wrath but also because of conscience."

Leslie Vernick says this about biblically responding to abuse:

1. It is good to protect yourself (Proverbs 27:12; Proverbs 11:9). David fled King Saul when he was violent toward him. The angel of the Lord warned Joseph to flee to Egypt with Jesus because Herod was trying to kill him. Paul escaped from those who sought to stone him. If you are being mistreated, and you have tried speaking up, standing up and setting boundaries and nothing has changed or stopped the abusive behavior, I believe it is biblically permissible to separate yourself from the abusive person in order to protect yourself from further harm.

2. It is good to expose the abuser (Ephesians 5:11) Sometimes we're very afraid to be bold and take a stand because then it lets other's know that our marriage is a mess and our spouse has been abusive. Bringing this out into the open is the ONLY way to get help for both yourself as well as your spouse. When things remain hidden, then a person can more easily stay self-deceived and blind to his/her own brokenness.

Also it is important to ask yourself if there is anything that you are doing to provoke and/or escalate a difficult or volatile situation. I have worked with couples where one spouse is trying to shut the conflict down because he or she is afraid of losing control, but the other spouse will not stop their arguing. The situation escalates and the one who feared losing control, does. I'm not excusing the abusive person in these cases, but sometimes we do create a situation where it is harder for someone to handle themselves in a godly way.

3. It is good to allow the violent person to experience the consequences of his/her sinful behavior. One of life's greatest teachers is consequences. God says what we sow, we reap (Galatians 6:7). A person uses violence at home because they can. God has put the civil authorities in place to protect victims of

abuse. The apostle Paul appealed to the Roman government when he was being mistreated (Acts 22:24-29).

When someone continually mistreats us, they lose the fellowship of our company. God does not ask us to have unconditional relationships with people even as he asks us to unconditionally love them. He calls us to love our enemies, not necessarily have fellowship with him/her. In a marital relationship what that means is that you will act in your spouses' best interests, even when that is difficult and costs you. (49)

2. Response to People Blaming You.

One thing that you may encounter and may sound reasonable is a version of this: "You are the one making him treat you this way. You are the one to blame. He wouldn't treat you like this if you weren't so ___."

This is what Lundy Bancroft says in response to a question during an interview with *Pandora's Project* about victim blaming:

> Kate: I have been told by therapists and also read (especially Dr Phil; but even Maya Angelou) that we teach people how to treat us. If this is true, how much of this is my fault? By staying wasn't I teaching the person that it was ok to continually treat me this way?
>
> LundyBancroft: These people are confusing abusers with other people. You can't significantly change an abuser's behavior. Leaving him is sometimes the best decision for you - that's a decision only you can make - but he will usually move on to find another woman to abuse. Maybe if a whole series of women leave him he'll start to change a little, but it tends to take more than that to make an abuser change — it tends to take arrest, prosecution, an abuser program, and (according to the research) a spell in jail.
>
> I'm sorry that those kinds of woman-blaming and victim-blaming theories get so much air time in the media. Women do need to find ways to take more power, but the path to power isn't by blaming yourself for falling in a trap that someone else had no business setting in the first place. I would also want to say to Dr. Phil, and to Maya Angelou, "You, and all communi-

ty members, contribute a lot to making it possible for abusers to get away with what they do, then you blame women for what happens.

If abused women share part of the responsibility, then their communities share even more of the responsibility for harboring abusers, letting them off the hook, buying into their excuses, supporting their mentality, and so forth. I don't think Dr. Phil and Maya Angelou would be so open to looking at THEIR contribution to the problem, would they? But they are happy to say that you should look at yours. As far as I'm concerned, the victims of a social tragedy are not the ones that should be assigned the primary responsibility to fix it. (50)

When you encounter victim blaming, a good response is to counter it with truth:

- Abuse is a conscious choice made by the abuser. They could walk away or communicate respectfully.

- Abuse is not about how the abuser was incited to hurt the victim, but rather feeling he is entitled to do what he wants to the victim.

- Reframe questions away from "why does the victim…" to "why does the perpetrator abuse?"

3. Response to His Claimed Repentance (signs it's authentic)

Developing new habits and new thinking patterns takes time to take root and show itself to be genuine. It will rarely be instant and lasting. Many abusers, if it suits their interests, can put on the appearance of being a new person for two or three years or more. Even if he claims a miraculous encounter with God that has completely changed him, you should remain skeptical and let time (a lot of time) tell the truth.

That does not mean you are doubting God, but that you are wise and cautious. God doesn't normally change a person's basic character and personality. Yes, he does deliver and set free, but it is still going to take time and effort to overcome old ways of thinking and behaving - old patterns and habits don't just go away overnight.

Sometimes Brian would get remorseful and declare that "As of this moment, I am a changed man! I will never let Satan into my life again. Never!" He would expect me to forget all his bad behavior and be thrilled that from then on he would "be the man of my dreams."

If he meant it when he said it, he did not put forth the effort toward change when the drama of the moment was over. The next few hours or days, as his enthusiasm faded, he went right back to his old ways. He would tell me to "be thankful I'm not like other men." (This shows the abuse cycle is still happening.)

<u>Signs he isn't really changing.</u>

Lundy Bancroft offers these signs that your abuser is not really changing:

- He tells you that you should be appreciating how much he has changed.
- He says "I can't be perfect" as an excuse to keep doing abusive things.
- He thinks it's okay to keep being abusive, as long as the incidents are farther apart than they used to be. (e.g. he says, "You are so upset with me, and I haven't done anything like that in a long time - I've been really good.")
- He tells you that now it's time for you to focus on the changes that you need to make.
- He is disconnecting from you emotionally — in other words, the reason he is being less abusive is that he is simply not being anything very much — he's withdrawn.
- He is continuing to make excuses.
- He says "We're getting along better." which means that as soon as you start to stand up to him or challenge him forcefully again, he'll be going right back to his old ways.
- He still gets impatient when you try to talk to him in a serious way about the things that are really important to you in life, including your desires for the relationship. (51)

<u>Evidence of authentic change:</u>

- He accepts responsibility for his choice to abuse you, and acknowledges that the abuse is wrong no matter what. That means no more excuses and blaming you or others for it.

- He understands and accepts that you are not his property and he does not have the right to control and dominate you. (This may be nearly impossible if he believes that God has made him master over you - tough to give up that lofty position!)

- He listens to, considers and respects your opinion even if he doesn't agree with it, and you feel safe to respectfully disagree with his. (For example, I desperately wanted furniture in our house rather than sitting on the floor. When Brian got some tax-refund money, I asked him very nicely if we could purchase an attractive used living room set that I had found on Craig's List. He pretended to listen and agree, but the next day bought a Holstein cow for me to milk because it fondly reminded him of the cows he had milked in prison. This is NOT showing respect or care!)

- He doesn't demand an "Atta boy!" every time he behaves well. (Brian's ego had to be constantly stroked which exhausted me - and his good behavior was short-lived anyway so not genuine change.)

- He will also not treat every good instance as a voucher to be spent on an occasional act of abuse: "I've been really good for a long time, why are you making such a big deal about it?"

- He stops coercing or forcing you to have sex. He shows consideration for your needs and desires. He respects your right to say "no."

- He will accept the natural consequences of his actions without blaming you, the children, others, or feeling sorry for himself. He also won't demand you fix it.

- He will change his response in highly heated environments. Whether it's another driver on the road, or your own frustration and anger, he will curb his own angry response.

- He will make an effort to identify patterns and attitudes that drive his abuse, and try to reduce or eliminate the triggers. As his wife, you will have good insight into this and he should ask for your perspective on what triggers him and not blow up at you for your insight.

- He understands that developing new thinking is a process that he will have to continually work on - it will not be instant. If it is 'instant', then you are still stuck in the cycle of abuse. But if it is genuine, then even when he falls, he will take responsibility, make amends, and do what he has to do to make things right with you and the children.

- He won't use his 'change' as a bargaining chip to control you: "I did this, so now it's time for you to do…"

- He will make an effort to carry his weight and share the power in the home.

- He will improve his parenting, his treatment of you as a parent, and will adjust his overall attitude toward all females to be respectful and considerate.

Does this sound lofty and out of reach? Actually, this is how normal healthy people act most of the time. Continual self-growth and consideration of others is normal. Abuse is not. If your husband is being genuine, it will become evident over time. Anyone can claim whatever they want, and even convince themselves of it. But only time, and subsequent actions when the pressure is on, will prove the veracity of it. If he gets angry at you for not being thrilled and convinced by his good behavior after the first two or three good episodes, then he clearly has NOT changed! You are still stuck in the cycle of abuse.

Pastor Jeff Crippen shows us from the Bible what genuine change looks like from the life of Saul of Tarsus:

But Christ can transform the chief of sinners - just as He laid hold of the murdering, persecuting Saul of Tarsus [Acts 9:1-9]. What will it look like? That is to say, what will happen - what will it look like - when an abuser is brought to genuine repentance? It will be traumatic - like no other trauma the man has probably ever experienced. When the bright, brilliant, penetrating and blinding light of Christ shines on him, such a man is going to suffer the trauma of realizing that everything he has been, all that he has thought, every goal he has pursued - the very grid and mindset through which he has perceived himself, other people, his victims, and God - ALL of it has been wrong! Radically, radically wrong. His mindset of power and control, of entitlement and of justification is going to come crashing down as Christ shows him his nothingness.

Consider again how this trauma of repentance evidenced itself in Paul - "9 But Saul, still breathing threats and murder against the disciples of the Lord, went to the high priest 2 and asked him for letters to the synagogues at Damascus, so that if he found any belonging to the Way, men or women, he might bring them bound to Jerusalem. 3 Now as he went on his way, he approached Damascus, and suddenly a light from heaven shone around him. 4 And falling to the ground he heard a voice saying to him, "Saul, Saul, why are you persecuting me?" 5 And he said, "Who are you, Lord?" And he said, "I am Jesus, whom you are persecuting. 6 But rise and enter the city, and you will be told what you are to do." 7 The men who were traveling with him stood speechless, hearing the voice but seeing no one. 8 Saul rose from the ground, and although his eyes were opened, he saw nothing. So they led him by the hand and brought him into Damascus. 9 And for three days he was without sight, and neither ate nor drank." (Acts 9:1-9 ESV)

And THAT is how it will be for the abusive man who is brought to true repentance in Christ. This is why we can be assured that the truly repentant man will cease from ALL blaming of others, he will cease from making excuses, he will be done with insisting on anything from others, including forgiveness, he will be entirely through with minimizing his sin, and he, who for his entire life viewed himself as a master, will now be humbled in the dust and become the slave of Christ and the servant of others. Where these changes are absent, there is NO real repentance. (52)

4. Grief

As a relationship comes to an end, even if it is ending only in the heart first, grief must be accepted as a normal part of the process of moving on to a better life. Long before I ever left Brian, I grieved the loss of my dreams of a happy life with him; the loss of the wonderful man I thought was the real him; the loss of a loving good dad for my daughters. I grieved the loss of other relationships and friendships; the loss of well-loved pets; the loss of my peace and joy. Through it, I didn't consciously understand I was grieving and that it was normal. All I knew was that the ache in my heart was deep and painful, relieved occasionally by spurts of happiness with Brian when he was remorseful (the honeymoon phase of the cycle of abuse).

After I left, I really needed to grieve the loss of the relationship through separation and divorce, but the stress of trying to survive without Brian did not allow any time for it. I stayed constantly on edge and stressed out. Thank God for people who stepped in and encouraged me to take some time for myself. This is one of the reasons it is so good to allow yourself to be open with others, such as in a dv support group. You will find allies and friends and you can encourage each other.

According to the Women's Resource Service in an article *Grief and Loss after Abuse*:

When a woman leaves an abusive relationship, family and friends will often celebrate the strength and courage it has taken for her to end the relationship. They are often genuinely relieved that she and the children are safer, and respond positively to her new life without him. Research shows that friends and family are less likely, however, to recognize the grief or loss a woman may also experience when a relationship ends, even though it has been abusive.

These losses may include:

Loss of a home and familiar environment

Loss of a partner who (usually) she once loved

Loss of the dream of a safe, respectful and loving partner

Loss of security, financial or emotional

Loss of a normal or desired family unit for children

Loss of a sense of identity, and/or their self-belief

Loss of relationships with family members of the ex-partner

Loss of their own good judgment capacities given that they are often held responsible for the abuse they endured.

This sense of loss can lead to feelings of intense grief. Although it is normal and natural, the process of grieving is quite hard and requires time, courage and support. (53)

Please allow yourself the right and time to grieve these losses. There is nothing wrong with you, and whatever you are feeling is legitimate. You don't have to apologize for it or explain yourself to anyone. It is an important stage to go through in order to move on to a healthy place. It helped me tremendously to join a support group. Even though I wasn't even considering a divorce when I joined, I was drawn to a divorce support group and found an invaluable group of people who accepted me and journeyed with me.

I would like to add here, that many women at this time turn to the church for support. Perhaps it will work for you, but as we talked about in chapter five, the church often blames the victim for what has happened. This only adds spiritual abuse on top of everything else you are going through. Your ex may even start attending and turn everyone against you.

However, many churches are getting trained in domestic violence and facilitating safe domestic violence support groups for victims and survivors. If you are looking for spiritual support along with domestic violence support, then these groups may be just what you are looking for. Ask around to see if anyone knows of such a group in your area. You can also call the churches and just ask directly if they have a "domestic violence support group."

I would encourage you to talk to your local shelter about dv support groups offered through them. Then you will know you are in a safe place where you can process at a comfortable pace and not fear judgment and condemnation.

Also important is to be honest with others about what you are going through. This honors yourself and what you have experienced. People may not respond helpfully, but by standing in truth, you will gain strength. You do not have to be ashamed. Your abuser should be ashamed. Don't take on his guilt for him. Hold him accountable for his choices.

Something else I did was to hold a type of private funeral to commemorate the loss of my dreams and my relationship. It was just between God and me, but it was extremely powerful to acknowledge the death of something significant in my life. I parted with the ring that symbolized that relationship. I had also written down a list of all the things that I was struggling with. So much heartache poured out in that list but it was buried with the ring. After a lot of tears and talking to God about it all, I left that "funeral" feeling cleansed and more ready to face the future. I continued to grieve - it is a process that can take a long time, but the finality of that "funeral" was an important part of healing.

Another thing that helps the grieving process is the awareness that the loss of a "normal" relationship and the loss of an "abusive" relationship are two different things altogether. You may research grief and find good resources to cope with the normal stages of it. But keep in mind that these are assuming the person you have lost was reasonably normal and healthy.

There are additional things that accompany the loss of a relationship with an abuser, and many people do not understand the complexity of your grief and that you can't just "move on" the same as can be done from a healthy relationship:

- Grief often includes the discovery of a web of lies on multiple levels.
- Coming to grips with understanding that you were only being used to serve the abusers self-serving agenda.
- When you hear about him in a new relationship, it brings anxiety about what the new woman/children are going to endure.
- Wondering if all that time with the abuser was a complete loss in your life.
- Wondering if he will reappear in your life and what chaos and destruction will result.
- Realizing that most people just don't understand how anyone could do the things you claim he did, which reinforces a sense of isolation and alienation.

Closure and a new self-awareness and strength is coming to you. You are not alone, and this part of your life has not been a waste. God can redeem and restore all that you feel has been wasted and lost. Romans 8:28 says "We know that all things work together for good for those who love God, who are called according to his purpose." Hold on to this promise through what seems utterly pointless and painful.

5. Forgiveness

What does forgiveness really mean? Does forgiveness mean I forget about everything that has happened with my abuser? Does it mean I have to stay with him or be reconciled to him? Why can't I forgive and FEEL like I have? Does my lingering anger mean I haven't really forgiven him?

Abuse victims are harangued about forgiving their abuser. These same people grant forgiveness and sympathy to the abuser, but withhold it from the victim themselves. Churches are particularly insidious in their favor of whoever appears to be the most believable and likable (inevitably the perpetrator), while condemning and often shunning the victim who is barely surviving. This just adds more confusion and oppression to victims - exactly the opposite of what Christ wants.

For a long time, after we left Brian, I was unable to forgive him and feel it inside. I would still feel angry and bitter. I wanted to just be able to forgive and forget, and to have peace. I wanted to move on with my life without constantly remembering him. However, thoughts about him would always start coming again, and my negative feelings would start building up like a pressure cooker.

It took me time to learn about the truth of forgiveness. There's no getting around that forgiveness without any exceptions is commanded in Scripture. Our eternal destiny depends on it: Matthew 6:14-15, "(14) For if you forgive others their trespasses, your heavenly Father will also forgive you; (15) but if you do not forgive others, neither will your Father forgive your trespasses."

Two things I learned that really helped me gain victory in this area are:

Forgiveness is an act of the will, nothing more.

I learned to CHOOSE forgiveness. I chose forgiveness because God required it for my own well-being. If God requires something of us, then he will do the work inside of us to accomplish what he wants if we are willing. God knows we are weak, and often we do not have the ability to obey him in our own power. That's why forgiveness is mostly an act of faith. As I came to understand that God was not asking me to feel anything, but rather to choose to align myself with his will, it became much easier to forgive. I stopped beating myself up for what I thought was my failure, and accepted that in the apparent imperfection of my choice, it was all God asked of me.

Often I said through gritted teeth with tears of rage rolling down my cheeks, "God, I CHOOSE to forgive Brian. But I have no feelings of peace and release to go with it. Honor my choice to obey you and somehow cause my feelings to line up with my choice."

I did this repeatedly, over many months. I never felt anything different at the time, but I just pushed through anyway and moved on with life until the next episode. But feelings are deceptive. One day I was out walking and enjoying a sunny peaceful day. As I walked and reflected on life, I suddenly realized, *Wow! I don't feel the anger toward Brian that I used to! In fact, I haven't even been thinking about him much!* I wasn't even quite sure when the last time was I had felt anything for him.

The sudden surprised recognition of peace in my heart toward Brian was a result of months, perhaps years, of God quietly healing me inside. Each time I chose forgiveness and asked God to work it out inside me, he did - as a process. And that's okay. Today I feel nothing toward Brian. I no longer have any feelings of anger that I have to deal with. I have no fear, no bitterness, and no regret. I have complete peace toward him and what happened.

The best kind of justice is God's justice.

Sometimes we have to let go of our right to exact revenge for abuse and injustice, and have faith in God that he will do what he says he will: Romans 12:19, "Beloved, never avenge yourselves, but leave room for the wrath of God; for it is written, 'Vengeance is mine, I will repay,' says the Lord."

As part of my healing process, I consoled myself that God would do exactly that - take vengeance on Brian. I was finally able to accept that I couldn't do it, but I sure was impatient for God to! I know full well how delightful it would be to help God along with that vengeance part! But it is not our place my friend. The Jewish Talmud offers the best advice: "Live well. It is the greatest revenge."

In time, I discovered that healing had not only produced peace toward Brian, but I had also lost the need for God's vengeance on him. Brian truly lost any place in my mind and heart. I know that God will deal with him - but he just is not my problem or concern any longer.

When you can reach this place of healing, you know that you are FREE. Allow yourself to travel this path with God, no matter how long it takes. God wants you to be at peace and to experience true freedom - the kind that only he can give. You were not made to carry the burden of the world's injustices on your shoulders. It is not your burden to figure out how and why each person should be punished.

Jesus says in Matthew 11:28-30, "(28) Come to me, all you that are weary and are carrying heavy burdens, and I will give you rest. (29) Take my yoke upon you, and learn from me; for I am gentle and humble in heart, and you will find rest for your souls. (30) For my yoke is easy, and my burden is light."

Don't let anyone beat you up over the forgiveness issue. Just be willing for God to work it out inside you. He will do it in his time and his way, and someday you will realize that your abuser no longer has a grip on you. When we are weak, God is strong. He is made perfect in our weakness.

Every time negative emotions and thoughts toward your (ex)husband threaten to overwhelm you, give them to God by faith. Not only will God work out peace in you, he will bring you joy. The joy of the Lord is your strength! I honestly don't know how he works this out in us, I just know he does.

2 Corinthians 12:9-10 "(9) but he said to me, 'My grace is sufficient for you, for power is made perfect in weakness.' So, I will boast all the more gladly of my weaknesses, so that the power of Christ may dwell in me. (10) Therefore I am content with weaknesses, insults, hardships, persecutions, and calamities for the sake of Christ; for whenever I am weak, then I am strong."

Reverend Marie Fortune shares on forgiveness of abusers in her book *Keeping the Faith: Questions and Answers for the Abused Woman*:

> Take heed to yourselves; if your brother sins, rebuke him, if he repents, forgive him; and if he sins against you seven times in the day, and turns to you seven times, and says, "I repent", you must forgive him. (Luke 17:1-4)
>
> First, Jesus says to take care of yourself. If someone abuses you (sins), rebuke him. In other words, somehow the abuser needs to hear that his behavior is wrong. This does not mean that you do it alone. It more likely means that you ask others to help you in that, perhaps the police or the pastor or other family members.
>
> Then, Jesus says, if he repents, forgive him. This is a big if. Repentance here means more than remorse. Remorse usually gets

expressed during the "making up" period of the battering cycle. The remorse may even be very genuine, but it does not mean that he will not hit again. Repentance is much more significant.

To repent, in both the Old and New Testaments, means to turn away from, to change, never to repeat again. True repentance on the part of the abuser means that he never hits again and that he learns to relate to you and/or other people in ways that are not controlling, demanding and dominating.

Forgiveness does not mean "forgiving and forgetting", implying that everything is fine now, pardoning the abuse or ignoring it. Forgiveness means putting that experience in perspective, putting it behind you and not allowing it to continue to victimize you. You can let go of it; you can remember it only when you need to. Forgiveness is for you, not for the abuser. His repentance, not your forgiveness, is what will finally bring about his healing. (54)

In the next and final chapter, we will look at how to overcome the giant of fear in our lives and how to experience a renewed loving relationship with God.

Chapter Seven
Freedom from Fear

The predominant underlying issue I battled through the years was fear. Even before I married Brian, I felt afraid of many things. Fear has a way of either paralyzing us so that we are indecisive when we need to take action, or pressuring us so that we make decisions quickly (which is normally unwise). Perhaps you can identify with some of the fears I felt:

- Fear of being alone caused me to jump recklessly into my marriage with Brian, ignoring all the red flags of a future abusive relationship.
- Fear of disappointing God caused me to submit to things I should never have submitted to.
- Fear of Brian caused me to stay quiet and not stand up to him.
- Fear of the future caused me to think I would never have it any better anyway.
- Fear of losing my children caused me to decide not to do anything to fight the abuse.
- Fear of unemployment, homelessness and not being able to provide for my children caused me to stay with Brian.
- Fear of being alone again.
- Fear of Brian's revenge if I did stand up to him or leave.
- Fear of Brian hurting the children.
- Fear that if I tried to hide he would find me.
- Fear of reaching out to others for any help or friendship - because Brian might hurt them.
- Fear of rejection and not being believed if I did speak up.

Fear produces other feelings - helplessness, hopelessness, despair, depression, confusion, and many more. Many of these fears are also contradictory which just increases the pain and paralysis. Once fear gets a grip, it doesn't let go easily.

The list I just gave has one common thread through it - everything is the opposite of God's way of doing and being. So if it is not of God, and it is not a natural instinct to imminent danger, then the other source is of the flesh or the demonic realm. Therefore, it is important to learn about and confront what is clearly a favorite tool of the enemy to keep us out of God's will.

"Fear not!" is the most repeated command in the Bible. God knows that Satan uses fear to overcome us, and he commands us to take an active role in resisting it. To be free of fear we must begin to eliminate the habits of fear-based thinking and relating with God and others. We have to learn to rely on the truth of God's Word.

There are two types of fear beyond the God-given instinct to flee danger: fear of God and a spirit of fear. Did you know that humans worship what they fear? Fear is an act of worship! In both the Hebrew and Greek, there are two words for worship. The first kind means to bow down, to kneel, and to put one's face down as an act of respect and submission. The attitude of the heart is essentially saying, "I will obey whatever you command of me." The other kind of word means to serve. Roughly, half of the time these words are translated as worship, and the other half as serve. They carry the idea of making a sacrifice or carrying out instructions. Worship involves three acts: speaking, listening, doing. Worship involves the mind and heart, and doing something. Think of this in connection with living with our abusers. Are we worshipping our abuser, and the one who is working through him (certainly not God!) Or, are we worshipping the Lord God?

Fear of God

Fear of God is a good thing and means respect and reverence of him because he is Creator, Master, Judge, King...and we are not. God alone is supreme and no one can stand against his decrees. The cosmos itself bows to him. However, God is not a cruel dictator ready to lower the boom every time we slip up. Instead, he is kind and patient with us. Fearing God holds many blessings and benefits such as wisdom, understanding, life, peace, contentment, joy, safety and security. (Psalm 111:10; Proverbs 1:7, 14:26-27, 19:23)

Proverbs 9:10 (AMP) says that "The [reverent] fear of the Lord [that is, worshiping Him and regarding Him as truly awesome] is the beginning and the preeminent part of wisdom [its starting point and its essence], And the knowledge of the Holy One is understanding and spiritual insight."

Spirit of Fear

The second type of fear is called a "spirit of fear." A spirit of fear brings destruction, torment and bondage and is from Satan and the kingdom of darkness.

2 Timothy 1:7 (AMP) says "For God did not give us a spirit of timidity or cowardice or fear, but [He has given us a spirit] of power and of love and of sound judgment and personal discipline [abilities that result in a calm, well-balanced mind and self-control]."

Whomever we set our thoughts upon the most, our heart's desire, our fear, our servitude - whoever sits on the throne of our heart is the one we are worshipping. When we need a miracle, we need to worship God.

When I woke up after sleeping on the beach in Chile, and went for a walk to talk to God and plead with him for help out of our desperate situation, he gave me a revelation of this. I wanted his help and blessing, but he was second place to Brian, and that was understandably not okay with him. I hadn't even realized over the years how Brian had usurped God's position on the throne of my heart. But indeed he had.

Before marrying Brian, even though I definitely had hang-ups and made mistakes, God was first place in my heart and mind. I loved God so much, thought about him often, talked to him frequently, and listened to him talk to me. I felt so in love with him, and completely loved back by him. All I wanted to do was please him. As long as I maintained this relationship with him, it seemed like life went smoothly and I enjoyed the blessings that come with an intimate relationship with God.

I also had a healthy respect for him. My friendship with him did not minimize the fact that he was God of the universe and I was not. In fact, the closer I felt to him, the more I recognized his holiness and my need for him as my Savior. There was absolutely no spirit of fear attached to it. The closer I walked with God, the less fear I felt, and the fewer mistakes I made in life.

1 John 4:18 (AMP) says "There is no fear in love [dread does not exist]. But perfect (complete, full-grown) love drives out fear, because

fear involves [the expectation of divine] punishment, so the one who is afraid [of God's judgment] is not perfected in love [has not grown into a sufficient understanding of God's love]."

When I slid backwards in my relationship with him, fear was at the door ready to step in and take up residence. When I met Brian, I ignored my God-given instincts warning me of danger. I justified Brian as God's will for my life. However, I did that because I was in a personal crisis and afraid of being alone. Rather than turning to God for peace and wisdom, I plunged forward driven by fear. The enemy had someone ready to step in and take me down a destructive path.

When I married Brian, I still thought that God was first place. In fact, Brian was very insistent that God be first place in our marriage and lives. But oh how deceptive and twisted the enemy of our souls can be! Fear does this - it warps our reasoning and ability to see truth clearly.

The reality was that Brian was serving a master other than God, no matter how much he proclaimed otherwise. Brian slowly replaced God in my mind, heart, and actions. I thought about Brian all the time - how could I please him, how could I be in his favor, what could I do for him, what did he want from me, and on and on. Only this "worship" produced the fruit of unrighteousness - fear, torment, compromise of values and constant worry. A spirit of fear had taken charge, and it was a harsh taskmaster.

The morning on the beach in Chile, God showed me that he needed to be put back on the throne of my heart. I needed to get my priorities straight spiritually before the rest of my miserable life could be repaired. Once I saw the truth of this, I gladly repented to him for my failure to worship and serve him alone.

I accepted that I had made choices that were driven by fear rather than faith - I couldn't blame Brian for all of it. Even though I thought my passivity was justified because of Brian, I realized that I had a free will and if I had faith in God, I never had to accept the treatment I received from Brian.

God calls his children to be proactive in abiding in truth and righteousness - never passive and accepting of whatever comes along. Passivity is from Satan to keep us in bondage so that we don't fulfill God's plan for our lives. There is a big difference between waiting because God is asking us to, and we have his peace; and being passive because we are paralyzed by fear.

God wanted me to put him first again, and be filled with peace and trust in him. When I repented and put God back on the throne of my heart, I didn't have a clue how anything would work out, but I had a deep sense of peace that I hadn't had in a long time. Fear was still there, trying to take back its seat of imminence, but I clung to God and resisted it the best I could anyway. God honored my obedience and faith, and did indeed rescue us in a miraculous way.

Overcoming fear in our lives is a process, and it doesn't mean fear ever stops trying to gain a foothold. The more deeply entrenched fear is, the more we may need support from other believers to help us gain victory. Look at the difference in the next two verses:

Psalm 56:3 (AMP) "When I am afraid, I will put my trust and faith in You."

Isaiah 12:2 (AMP) "Behold, God, my salvation! I will trust and not be afraid, For the Lord God is my strength and song; Yes, He has become my salvation."

The first writer acknowledges fear has already taken hold, but chooses to resist and trust in the Lord. In the second one, the writer's faith has matured to the point that trust is dominant and fear does not even gain an entry. Our faith in Jesus grows, matures, and keeps us from fear. Psalm 27:1, "The Lord is my light and my salvation; whom shall I fear? The Lord is the stronghold of my life; of whom shall I be afraid?"

Turning on our faith is like turning on a light in a dark room. When we walk into a dark room, we do not try to shoo out the darkness or fight it with our fists. We just turn on the light and the darkness flees. Faith is the light switch that causes the darkness of fear to flee. We get faith by being filled with the Word of God on a regular basis and proclaiming its truths over our lives: Romans 10:17, "So faith comes from what is heard, and what is heard comes through the word of Christ." James 4:7, "Submit yourselves therefore to God. Resist the devil, and he will flee from you."

It is important to realize that the devil does have certain power. Most of his power is wielded through fear. However, Jesus calls him a liar when he speaks to the hypocritical religious leaders in John 8:44 (AMP) "You are of your father the devil, and it is your will to practice the desires [which are characteristic] of your father. He was a murderer from the beginning, and does not stand in the truth because there is no truth in him. When he lies, he speaks what it natural to him, for he is a liar and the father of lies and half-truths."

The power of God is much greater than the power of Satan. It is much greater than the power of those who serve the kingdom of darkness.

1 John 4:4 (AMP), "Little children (believers, dear ones), you are of God and you belong to Him and have [already] overcome them [the agents of the antichrist]; because He who is in you is greater than he (Satan) who is in the world [of sinful mankind]."

All of hell and Satan himself is subject to the power of Jesus. Matthew 28:18, "And Jesus came and said to them, "All authority in heaven and on earth has been given to me."

You are not stronger than the devil, but Jesus is. When fear and worry attacks you, you can pray in the name of Jesus, resist and overcome it. Luke 10:19 (AMP), "Listen carefully: I have given you authority [that you now possess] to tread on serpents and scorpions, and [the ability to exercise authority] over all the power of the enemy (Satan); and nothing will [in any way] harm you."

This authority is yours if you belong to him, believe his Word and pray in his name. The Bible speaks of the power of coming into agreement with other believers. Deuteronomy 32:30, "How could one have routed a thousand, and two put a myriad to flight, unless their Rock had sold them, the Lord had given them up?" Matthew 18:19 (AMP) "Again I say to you, that if two believers on earth agree [that is, are of one mind, in harmony] about anything that they ask [within the will of God], it will be done for them by My Father in heaven."

If you do not regularly pray Scripture, you may like to start by using what I pray over myself and my family. I compiled some of them in Appendix A and personalize them using names and places. Your children may be in another home so personalize verses to that situation. You may be going through legal battles and having to deal with different agencies. Perhaps you are in hiding, or still live with your abuser. No matter what obstacle you are facing, no matter what your greatest fear is, God is bigger - Luke 1:37, "For nothing will be impossible with God."

What is important is to build and maintain a relationship with God through praying his Word over yourself and your family. The more you meditate on and pray God's Word, faith will get bigger and fear and torment will lose its grip on you. Ask God to give you a promise from his Word to sustain you. He will do it! Then hold onto it and believe it.

Whenever fear and doubt come to your mind, speak out the Word to counteract it. This is showing who your faith is in and who you are choosing to worship. Put God first place every day and actively resist what Satan brings against you. You will see situations start to turn around that previously seemed impossible. Things might not go exactly the way you think they should, but God in his wisdom will work all things for good. You will be able to see that in hindsight. Trust in God is never misplaced.

I want to thank you, dear reader, for spending time with me in the pages of this book. I hope that something here has touched your heart and given hope and inspiration to you to continue to move forward. Do not give up! One day the trials you are enduring really will end. Perhaps you will find ways, as I have, to come alongside others and help them through their pain. We need each other for strength and encouragement. In the hands of God, your life is not over, your purpose is not extinguished, your past is not wasted, and your children are not lost. I pray for God's blessings on you and your children, his peace to envelope you, and his joy to strengthen you!

Isaiah 57:15 "For thus says the high and lofty one who inhabits eternity, whose name is Holy: I dwell in the high and holy place, and also with those who are contrite and humble in spirit, to revive the spirit of the humble, and to revive the heart of the contrite."

Appendix A
Scriptures for Prayer and Meditation

(1 John 5:14-15) Thank you Father, for the confidence, assurance and privilege of boldness, which I have in you. I know that if I ask anything or make any request according to your will you listen to and hear me. And since I know that you listen to me in whatever I ask according to your Word, I also know with settled and absolute knowledge that I have granted to me as my present possessions the requests I make of you.

(Mark 11:24; I John 5:14-15) Thank you for your promise that whatever I ask for in prayer, believing, it is granted to me. Therefore, I receive as my present possession the things which I am praying for, being fully assured that as I am praying your Word, I am praying your will.

(Isaiah 55:11) Thank you that as your Word goes out of my mouth, it is not returning to you void or useless without producing any effect, but it is accomplishing that which you please and purpose, and it is prospering in the thing for which you sent it.

(John 14:13; Psalm 138:2) Thank you Father, that as I pray your Word, you have promised that you will do - you yourself will grant - whatever I ask in your name, so that you will be glorified and extolled through your Son. You have also said that you have exalted above all else your name and your Word, and that you have magnified your Word above all your name! So Father, I not only pray in the name of Jesus today, but I pray your Word, knowing that you will honor your word even above all your name.

Children

(Hebrews 13:20-21) Thank you Father, that you, the God of peace, are strengthening, completing, perfecting and making my children what they ought to be. You are equipping them with everything good that they may carry out your will; while you yourself work in them and accomplish that which is pleasing in your sight.

(Isaiah 11:2-4) Thank you Father that your Holy Spirit rests upon my children; the spirit of wisdom and understanding, the spirit of counsel and might, the spirit of knowledge and the reverential and obedient fear of the Lord. You are making them of quick understanding, and their delight is in the reverential and obedient fear of the Lord. They do not judge by the sight of their eyes, neither do they decide by the hearing of their ears, but they judge with righteous judgment.

(Colossians 1:9-11) Father, I declare that my children are being filled with the full, deep and clear knowledge of your will, in all spiritual wisdom into your ways and purposes; and in understanding and discernment of spiritual things. They are walking, living and conducting themselves in a manner worthy of you, fully pleasing to you, and desiring to please you in all things. They are bearing fruit in every good work, and steadily growing and increasing in the knowledge of you. They are being invigorated and strengthened with all power according to the might of your glory, and exercising every kind of endurance and patience with joy.

(Ezekiel 16:60; Isaiah 14:24, 27; Proverbs 19:2; Psalm 33:9-11) Thank you Father that you are earnestly remembering your covenant with my children and you are establishing an everlasting covenant with them. As you have thought and planned concerning my children, so shall it happen. As you have purposed for my children, so shall it stand; for what you have purposed, who can annul it? When your hand is stretched out, who will turn it back? What you speak is done. What you command stands fast. You bring the counsel of corrupt people to nothing; you make the thoughts and plans of wicked people to no effect. Your counsel stands forever; the thoughts of your heart to all generations. My children have many plans in their minds, and other people may have plans for them, but it is your purpose for them that will stand.

(Isaiah 54:10, 9:6; Psalm 57:2, 138:8; Philippians 1:6) Thank you Father that you have cut a covenant of peace and completeness with my children that shall never be removed. Jehovah Shalom, you rule and reign as the God of Peace wherever my children are. You began a good work in them and are perfecting and completing that which concerns them. My children are crying to you O God, the one who performs on their behalf and rewards them. You bring to pass your purposes for them and surely complete them.

(Ephesians 3:16-19) Thank you Father, that you are granting out of the rich treasury of your glory, that my children be strengthened and reinforced with mighty power in their inner selves by the Holy Spirit indwelling their innermost beings and personalities. Christ, through their faith, is making his permanent home in their hearts. They are being rooted deep in love and founded securely on love. Therefore, they have the power and are strong to apprehend and grasp with all the saints, the experience of that love - the breadth and length and height and depth of it. They are really coming to know, practically, through experience for themselves, the love of Christ, which far surpasses mere knowledge without experience. As a result, they are being filled through all their being unto all your fullness. They have the richest measure of your Divine Presence, and have become wholly filled and flooded with you.

(Ephesians 1:17-19) Thank you Father, that you have granted my children a spirit of wisdom and revelation in the knowledge of you, by having the eyes of their hearts flooded with light, so that they can know and understand the hope to which you have called them, and how rich is their inheritance in the saints, and so that they can know and understand what is the immeasurable, unlimited and surpassing greatness of your power in and for them.

(2 Timothy 1:7-8) Thank you Father, that you have not given my children a spirit of fear, but of power, authority, love, a calm well-balanced mind, discipline and self-control. They do not shrink back in shame to testify for you and for the truth.

(Zephaniah 3:9; Joshua 24:15) Thank you Father for changing my family's impure language and giving to us a clear and pure speech from pure lips. We are calling on your name, serving you with one unanimous consent and one united shoulder, bearing the yoke of the Lord. As for me and my house, we are serving you Lord.

Purity

(1 Thessalonians 4:3-5) Father, I declare that my children are consecrated, separated and set apart for pure and holy living. They abstain and shrink from all sexual vice. They each know how to possess,

control and manage their own bodies in purity, separated from things profane and in consecration and honor. Their bodies are not used in the passion of lust, either theirs or anyone else's.

(Psalm 140:1-5) Protect my children, Father God. Preserve my children from violent men, who plan evil things in their hearts and whose speech is as the venom of vipers. Give me and my children discernment over who these people are who don't know you. Guard my children from those who would plan to snare them in their nets. I pray a hedge of protection over my children.

Harmony

(Philippians 2:1-3) Father, fill up our dwelling with your peace and joy. May we live in harmony with each other, having the same mind and purpose. Help us to not do anything from selfishness, strife or for unworthy ends, but instead with a true spirit of humility regard each other as better than ourselves, showing affection and compassionate sympathy.

(1 Peter 3:8) Thank you Father, for bringing my family into one and the same mind, that we sympathize with each other, loving each other, compassionate and courteous toward each other.

(2 Corinthians 2:11; Ephesians 4:29-32) Father, I declare that my family lets no foul language, nor evil word, nor unwholesome talk come out of our mouths; but only such speech as is good and beneficial to the spiritual progress of others, as is fitting to the need and the occasion, that it may be a blessing and give grace to those who hear it. We do not grieve the Holy Spirit by whom we were sealed. We let all bitterness, wrath, passion, rage, bad temper, resentment, anger, animosity, quarrelling, brawling, clamor, contention, slander, evil-speaking, abusive or blasphemous language be banished from us, with all malice, spite, ill will or baseness of any kind. We have become useful, helpful and kind to one another; tenderhearted, compassionate, understanding, forgiving one another readily and freely as you in Christ forgave us, in order that Satan get no advantage over us; for we are not ignorant of his wiles and intentions.

Rebellion

(Jeremiah 29:22-24) Father, I declare that I am not ashamed, nor is my face pale with fear and disappointment because of my children's degeneracy. For I see my children walking in the ways of piety and virtue, with the work of your hands in my midst. They revere your name; they revere the Holy one of Jacob and reverently fear the God of Israel. Those who erred in spirit are coming to understanding, and those who murmured discontentedly are accepting instruction.

Parenting

(Philippians 4:13) I can do all things through Christ Jesus who strengthens me and gives me sufficiency for every task.

(Philippians 4:6-7) I will not fret or have any anxiety about anything, but in every circumstance and in everything by prayer and thanksgiving, will make my requests known to God. Thank you Father for your peace that transcends all understanding - that it guards my heart and mind in Christ Jesus.

(1 Peter 5:2-3) Father, I declare that I tend, nurture, guard, guide and fold my children; not by coercion or constraint, but willingly; not dishonorably motivated by the advantages belonging to me as a parent, but eagerly and cheerfully. Not as an arrogant, dictatorial and overbearing person, domineering over my children, but being an example, pattern and model of Christian living and Christ's love to them.

(Malachi 4:5-6; Ephesians 6:1-3; 2 Thessalonians 3:4) Father, I declare that the Spirit of Elijah is turning and reconciling, through repentance, the hearts of my children to me, and my heart to them. Therefore, my children obey me in the Lord. They honor, esteem and value me as precious, and as a result, all is well with them and they shall live long on the earth. I have confidence that my children are doing and will continue to do the things I wisely suggest and charge them to do.

(John 6:28-29; Jeremiah 31:16-17) Thank you Father, that the only work which you require of me as a mother is to believe in your son Jesus. Therefore, I claim your promise that my work shall be rewarded. By faith, I declare that my children are returning from the enemy's land. There is hope in my future. My children are coming again to their own country.

Victory

(Psalm 55:18,22) Thank you Father for ransoming my children and myself unharmed from the battle waged against us. I cast all my cares upon you and thank you for sustaining us.

(Ezekiel 22:30; Isaiah 58:6; Matthew 18:18; Psalm 34:7) I build up the wall and stand in the gap on behalf of my children. I loose the chains of injustice and untie the cords of the yoke to set the oppressed free and break every yoke. I bind all the powers of darkness that come against my children and me and I loose the powers of the kingdom of God in our lives. Thank you that the angel of the Lord encamps around us and delivers us.

(Psalm 112:7, 34:9-10; Proverbs 3:26) I thank you Father that I lack no good thing. You are my confidence and will keep my foot, and my children's feet, from being snared. I will not fear bad news because my heart is steadfast, trusting in you.

(2 Corinthians 6:14) Father, I declare that my children do not unequally yoke themselves up with unbelievers. They do not come under a different yoke with those whose lives are inconsistent with their faith. If my children are put under a yoke of bondage, I trust you to protect them and set them free from it.

(2 Timothy 2:25-26; Proverbs 13:20; 1 Corinthians 15:33-34) Father, I ask you to deliver my children from corrupt and evil companions and influences. Bring them to the knowledge of the truth and help them escape out of the snare of the devil that has held them captive so that they may do your will. May my children walk as companions of the wise and therefore be wise.

(Hebrew 4:7) Father, I pray that when my children hear your voice, and hear truth, they do not harden their hearts. Open their eyes to what is truth and protect them from lies and deception.

(John 14:26) Thank you Holy Spirit, that you are teaching my children all things and leading them into all truth. You are causing them to recall, reminding them, and bringing to their remembrance everything that is of truth.

(Isaiah 54:13-17) Father, I declare that all of my children are disciples, taught of you and obedient to your will. Great is their peace and undisturbed composure. They are establishing themselves on righteousness. They are far even from the thought of oppression or destruction. They do not fear. They are far from terror, for it does not come near them. He who stirs up strife against them and me is failing away to us. No weapon that is formed against us is prospering. Every tongue that rises against us in judgment we are showing to be in the wrong.

(Psalm 102:28; Isaiah 49:25) Father, I declare that my children dwell safely and continue, and their descendants shall be established before you. You are contending with him who contends with me, and you are granting safety, saving and easing my children.

(Acts 5:38-39) Father, I declare that every purpose or undertaking that is of human or demonic origin in our lives is failing, being overthrown and coming to nothing. Every purpose or undertaking that is of YOU cannot be stopped, overthrown or destroyed.

Protection

(2 Corinthians 10:4; Revelation 12:11; Matthew 6:14; 1 John 1:9) By faith I pull down every stronghold I have yielded to Satan and claim by faith that it is canceled and covered under the blood of Jesus. Thank you Father for forgiving me and cleansing me of my sins when Christ died on the cross.

(James 4:6-7; 1 Peter 5:6-9; Matthew 16:19; Revelation 7:1; Hosea 2:6; Zechariah 2:5) I submit myself under the authority of the Lord Jesus Christ and I bind all demonic forces that are trying to hinder me and my children from being in the will of God. I claim by faith that we are surrounded by a hedge of protection, a wall of fire, and a wall of faith all covered under the blood of Jesus.

(Hebrew 1:14; Romans 6:4; Ephesians 5:18; Matthew 18:18; John 16:13) I bind all demonic forces by the blood of the Lamb and pray that Jesus would send holy angels to stop any evil assignment against my children and myself. By faith I release the working power of the resurrected Lord and the Holy Spirit in our lives. By faith I claim that every evil assignment has been bound in heaven and thank you that you will guide us into the center of your will and show us the works you have planned for us.

(Psalm 35:4, 26; 1 Corinthians 15:57; Luke 6:38; Ephesians 1:17-19; Galatians 5:22-23) Father, I thank you for causing confusion in the camp of mine enemies so that I may have victory over them. Thank you for victory over every trial. Send your messengers and the provision that I need to accomplish your will. Give me knowledge and wisdom to know and do your will. Fill me with the power of the Holy Spirit and give me the fruit of the Spirit to accomplish your will.

(Psalm 118:17) Father, I declare that my children and I shall not die, but live, and declare your works and illustrious acts.

(Isaiah 32:18) I declare that my children and I dwell in a peaceable habitation, in a safe dwelling and in a quiet resting place.

(Psalm 32:8; II Timothy 4:18) Thank you Father that you are instructing my children and I and teaching us in the way that we should go. You are counseling us with your eye upon us. You are delivering and drawing us unto yourself from every assault of evil. You are preserving and bringing us safe to your heavenly kingdom.

(Psalm 91:9-16) Father, because I have made you my dwelling place and my refuge, I trust that no evil shall befall my children or me, that no plague will come near our dwelling place. Command your angels to guard us and bear us up. In your strength, we will tread upon the lion and adder. As a mother of your children, I rest on your promise, "I will rescue those who love me. I will protect those who trust in my name. When they call on me I will answer; I will be with them in trouble. I will rescue and honor them. I will reward them with long life and give them my salvation."

Provision

(1 John 3:22; John 15:7) I receive from God whatever I ask of him because I watchfully and habitually practice what is pleasing to him. I live in him and his words are in my heart, therefore I ask whatever I will and it will be done for me.

(Psalm 84:11; Philippians 4:6-7, 19) The Lord is my sun and shield and he bestows grace, favor and honor on me. No good thing does he withhold from me because I walk uprightly. He liberally supplies all my needs according to his riches in glory in Christ Jesus. I bring everything to him in prayer with thanksgiving, and the peace of God, which passes all understanding, keeps my heart and mind through Christ Jesus.

Healing

(Isaiah 53:4-5) Thank you Jesus for bearing my grief and carrying my sorrow. You were stricken, smitten of God and afflicted that I may have life. You were wounded for my transgressions and bruised for my iniquities. The chastisement of my peace was upon you, and by your stripes I am healed. I receive Jesus as my Healer just as I have received him as my Savior. The power to resist sickness resides in me.

(2 Peter 1:4; Matthew 8:17) I walk in divine health and life, for Jesus has conquered sickness in my life. Thank you Jesus for taking my sickness on your body, and that by your suffering I am healed. Divine health pulsates through every cell of my body, overcoming sickness and disease.

(Jeremiah 17:14; Matthew 10:1; Psalm 41:1-3) Heal me Lord, and I shall be healed; save me and I shall be saved, for you are my praise. I thank you that it is your will that in my life every unclean spirit is cast out, and every disease and affliction is healed. You deliver me in the day of trouble; you protect me and keep me alive. You do not give me up to the will of my enemies. You sustain me through sickness and restore me to full health.

(Jeremiah 33:6; Psalm 103:2-4) Thank you Father for healing my broken heart and binding up my wounds. You bring me health and healing and reveal to me abundance of prosperity and security. I will not forget you and all your benefits. You forgive me all my iniquity, heal all my diseases, redeem my life from destruction, and crown me with your steadfast love and mercy.

Courage

Deuteronomy 31:6-8; 2 Timothy 1:7) Thank you Father for giving me strength and boldness. I will not live in fear or dread, because you go with me everywhere I go and I have confidence that you will never fail me nor forsake me. I will be strong and courageous. I will not come under the dominion of fear and dismay, for you did not give me a spirit of fear and timidity, but a spirit of power, love and a strong mind.

(Joshua 1:9-10; 1 Corinthians 16:13) Because I love and worship you alone God, I can be strong and courageous to face every battle in front of me. I will not be terrified or discouraged, for you are with me wherever I go. I am on my guard, standing firm in my faith in you, a woman of great courage and strength and wisdom.

(Proverbs 3:5; Psalm 112:7) I trust in the Lord with all my heart and do not rely on my own understanding. In all my ways I acknowledge him and he makes my paths straight. I have no fear of bad news. My heart is steadfast, trusting in the Lord.

Peace

(Psalm 4:8, 85:8,10, 119:165) I will lie down and sleep in peace; for you alone Lord make my children and me lie down in safety. You speak peace to us because I am faithful to you and turn to you with all my heart. Your steadfast love, faithfulness, righteousness and peace fill us and surround us. Because I love you, I abide in great peace and nothing can make me stumble.

(Proverbs 16:7; Isaiah 26:3) Thank you Father for causing me to please you and that you cause my enemies to be at peace with me. You ordain peace for me and keep my mind in perfect peace because I trust in you.

(Isaiah 32:17-18) You lead me in paths of righteousness and cause my children and I to dwell in a peaceful habitation, in secure dwellings and in quiet resting places. We enjoy the result of righteousness which is quietness and trust forever.

(Isaiah 54:10-12) Thank you Father that though the mountains may depart and the hills be removed, your steadfast love and covenant of peace shall not be removed from my children or I. You have compassion on us and lead us forth in joy and back in peace.

Appendix B
Warning Signs of Abuse

The following questions ask you about your relationship. If you are not currently in a relationship, these are signs or "red flags" to assist you in identifying a potentially abusive person.

- Do you feel nervous around your partner?
- Do you have to be careful to control your behavior to avoid your partner's anger?
- Do you feel pressured by your partner when it comes to sex?
- Are you scared of disagreeing with your partner?
- Does your partner criticize you, or humiliate you in front of other people?
- Is your partner always checking up on you or questioning you about what you do without your partner?
- Does your partner control where you go or check the mileage on your car?
- Does your partner repeatedly and wrongly accuse you of seeing or flirting with other people?
- Does your partner tell you that if you changed, he or she wouldn't treat you like this?
- Does your partner's jealousy stop you from seeing friends or family?
- Does your partner make you feel like you are wrong, stupid, crazy, or inadequate?
- Has your partner ever scared you with violence or threatening behavior?
- Does your partner throw or break objects to intimidate you?
- Does your partner make you feel scared by driving too fast and refusing to slow down when you ask?
- Does your partner say, "I will kill myself if you break up with me" or "I will hurt/kill you if you break up with me"?

- Does your partner make excuses for the abusive behavior? For example: saying, "It's because of alcohol or drugs," or "I can't control my temper," or "I was just joking"?
- Does your partner brag about bullying or harming others or animals?
- Has your partner abused or killed your animals?
- Does your partner impose stereotypical gender roles?

Courtesy of Center for Relationship Abuse Awareness

You do not deserve to be abused. Create a safety plan (Appendix D) or call someone to talk about your relationship. You may also want to contact the National Domestic Violence Hotline at (800) 799-SAFE to be connected to a local organization.

Appendix C
Risk Assessment

There is a free MOSAIC threat assessment here: www.mosaicmethod.com/. The MOSAIC method works by breaking a situation down to its elements and then seeing what picture emerges when the pieces of the puzzle are put together.

Abusive relationships often become more violent over time. While it is impossible to predict with any degree of certainty when relationships will escalate to lethal violence, researchers have identified some common factors. Lack of the following circumstances does not necessarily indicate that violence will not become lethal. Abused women should always use extreme care in planning for safety and should rely on their own instincts in determining appropriate responses to violent situations. Although lethality assessments can be useful, you are the best judge of the danger your batterer poses to you and your children.

Lethality Assessment Factors

- Threats of Suicide or Murder: In the vast majority of cases were women are killed, the perpetrator has first threatened her life or his own. A suicide threat should be taken very seriously. In many cases, men murder their wives and children, and then commit suicide. The more specific a threat, the more seriously it should be viewed.

- Availability of Weapons: A risk of lethal violence has also been associated with the batterer's possession of or access to weapons, the use of weapons or threats of such use in prior incidents and escalation of the violence in frequency or severity.

- Controlling and Jealous Behavior: A risk of lethal violence is associated with an increase in controlling or jealous behavior.

Such behavior can include following her, demanding to know where she is at all times or restricting her movement.

- Use of Drugs and Alcohol: Alcohol may reduce inhibitions to use lethal violence or prevent a batterer from adequately understanding the lethal nature of the force he is using.

- Depression: The mental health of the man can indicate his propensity for lethal violence. If a man has lost hope and "given up" he is more likely to cause serious injury or death.

- Batterer's Isolation: Studies indicate that the isolation of the batterer and the extent to which he is dependent on the battered woman correlate with the use of lethal violence.

- Escalation of Violence: Studies also indicate that escalation of the violence in frequency or severity can also indicate increased dangerousness.

- End of the Relationship: Research indicates that the most dangerous time for a battered woman is after she ends the relationship. In the United States, some statistics show that women who leave their batterers are at a 75% greater risk of being killed by their batterers than those who stay. It is very important for a battered woman to make her own decision to leave a relationship because she is in the best position to assess the potential danger.

- Choking or Strangling: Legal professionals have identified the abuser's prior "choking" or "strangling" of the victim as an indicator of extreme danger.

Modified from Minnesota Advocates for Human Rights

Appendix D
Safety Plan

<u>If you had the perpetrator evicted or are living alone, you may want to:</u>
- Change locks on doors and windows.
- Install a security system — window bars, locks, better lighting, smoke detectors and fire extinguishers.
- Teach the children to call the police or family and friends if they are snatched.
- Talk to schools and childcare providers about who has permission to pick up the children.
- Find a lawyer knowledgeable about family violence to explore custody, visitation and divorce provisions that protect you and your children.
- Obtain a restraining order.

<u>If you are leaving the abuser, consider the following:</u>
- How and when can you most safely leave? Where will you go?
- Are you comfortable calling the police if you need them?
- Who can you trust to tell that you are leaving?
- How will you travel safely to and from work or school or to pick up children?
- What community and legal resources will help you feel safer? Write down their addresses and phone numbers, and keep them handy.
- Do you know the number of the local shelter?
- What custody and visitation provisions will keep you and your children safe?
- Is a restraining order a viable option?
- Open a savings account in your own name. Give the bank a safe address, like a post office box or your work address.

- Leave money, an extra set of keys, and copies of your important papers with someone you trust. You may need to leave home fast, and you'll need these things later.

If you are staying with the abuser, think about:
- What works best to keep you safe in an emergency.
- Who you can call in a crisis.
- If you would call the police if the violence starts again. Can you work out a signal with the children or the neighbors to call the police when you need help?
- If you need to flee temporarily, where would you go? Think through several places where you can go in a crisis. Write down the addresses and phone numbers, and keep them with you.
- If you need to flee your home, know the escape routes in advance.
- Have the following available in case you have to flee: Important papers such as birth certificates, social security cards, marriage and driver's licenses, car title, lease or mortgage papers, passports, insurance information, school and health records, welfare and immigration documents, and divorce or other court documents; credit cards, bank account number, and ATM cards; some money; an extra set of keys; medications and prescriptions; phone numbers and addresses for family, friends, doctors, lawyers, and community agencies; clothing and comfort items for you and the children.

Before and during an attack do the following:
- Stay close to a door or window so you can get out if you need to.
- Stay away from the bathroom, the kitchen, and weapons.
- Practice your escape. Know which doors, windows, elevator, or stairs would be best.
- Have a packed bag ready. Hide it in a place that you can get to quickly.
- Identify neighbors you can tell about the violence. Ask them to call the police if they hear signs of domestic violence coming from your home.
- Have a "code word" to use with your children, family, friends, and neighbors. Ask them to call the police when you say that word.

- Know where to go if you have to leave home, even if you don't think you'll have to.
- Trust your instincts. Do whatever you have to do to survive.

At work, you may want to:

- Save any threatening emails or voicemail messages. You can use these to take legal action in the future, if you choose to. If you already have a restraining order, the messages can serve as evidence in court that the order was violated.
- Park close to the entrance of your building, and talk with security, the police, or a manager if you fear an assault at work.
- Have your calls screened, transfer harassing calls to security, or remove your name and number from automated phone directories.
- Relocate your workspace to a more secure area.
- Obtain a restraining order and make sure that it is current and on hand at all times. Include the workplace on the order. A copy should be provided to the police, the employee's supervisor, Human Resources, the reception area, the Legal department, and Security.
- Provide a picture of the perpetrator to reception areas and/or Security.
- Identify an emergency contact person should the employer be unable to contact you.
- Ask Security to escort you to and from your car or public transportation.
- Look into alternate hours or work locations.
- Review the safety of your childcare arrangements, whether it is on-site childcare at the company or off-site elsewhere. If you have a restraining order, it can usually be extended to the childcare center.

Remember, you cannot stop your partner's abuse; but you can find help and support for yourself. No one deserves to be abused.

Courtesy of Futures Without Violence

Appendix E
Safety-Packing Checklist

If you are leaving an abusive situation, take your children and, if possible, your pets. Put together the items listed below. Hide them someplace where you can get them quickly, or leave them with a friend. If you are in immediate danger, though, leave without these items.

<u>Identification for yourself and your children</u>

    Birth certificates
    Social Security cards (or numbers written on paper if you can't find the cards)
    Driver's license
    Photo identification or passports
    Welfare benefits card
    Green card

<u>Important papers</u>

    Marriage certificate
    Divorce papers
    Custody orders
    Legal protection or restraining orders
    Health insurance papers and medical cards
    Medical records for all family members
    Children's school records
    Investment papers/records and account numbers
    Work permits
    Immigration papers
    Rental agreement/lease or house deed
    Car title, registration, and insurance information
    Records of police reports you have filed or other evidence of abuse

<u>Money and other ways to get by</u>

Cash
  Credit cards
  ATM card
  Checkbook and bankbook (with deposit slips)
  Jewelry or small objects you can sell

<u>Keys</u>

  House
  Car
  Safety deposit box or Post Office box

<u>Ways to communicate</u>

  Phone calling card
  Cell phone
  Address book
  (It is best not to use a card or phone that you shared with an abuser because he or she may be able to use them to find you.)

<u>Medications</u>

  At least one month's supply for all medicines you and your children are taking
  A copy of any prescriptions

<u>Things to help you cope</u>

  Pictures
  Keepsakes
  Children's small toys or books

Courtesy the Office on Women's Health

Appendix F
Technology Safety

For more in-depth information, visit the National Network to End Domestic Violence.

The NNEDV also has a particularly good pdf on *Technology Safety Quick Tips* for each device such as: computer and phone monitoring software, keystroke logging hardware, GPS Devices, Cell and Mobile Phones, Caller ID and Spoofing, Faxes, Cordless Phones, TTY, Relay Services, Email, Hidden Cameras, and Personal Information on the Internet.

Another particularly good article on tech safety is at the Minnesota Center against Violence and Abuse. It's called "A High-Tech Twist on Abuse: Technology, Intimate Partner Stalking, and Advocacy."

Technology is ever changing, and it can be used to jeopardize your safety or as a means to keep you safe. Since power and control issues are a part of domestic violence, abusive partners frequently use technology to monitor and control those they abuse. Here are some things to keep in mind as you use technology.

> Do you have a feeling that you are being monitored?
>
> Did you know that someone can monitor another person's computer use without the user knowing?
>
> Did you know that a "history" cannot be completely erased from a computer?
>
> Did you know that cell phone use can be monitored?
>
> Did you know that a global positioning system (GPS) can be placed on your car, in your purse or in your cell phone?
>
> Did you know that some court systems are placing court records online and that they may contain personal information?

Did you know that e-mail is like a postcard and can be intercepted?

Ways to Ensure your Safety

Internet Safety

As you surf the internet, the places you visit are stored on the computer you use. Bills you pay and purchases you make are tracked. Instant messages and emails can be retrieved. Keep in mind that as you use a computer, it might be monitored. Safe computers can be found at the local library, internet café, shelter, work or computer technology center. Always use safe computers when researching things such as travel plans, housing options, legal issues and safety plans.

Email

Your abusive partner could have access to your email account. To be safe, open an email account your partner does not know about on a safe computer and use that account for safety planning and sensitive communications. It is a good idea to keep your monitored account active with non-critical emails in order to maintain appearances.

Cell Phone

Cell phones can be a beacon, tracking your exact location in real time. Call and text history can also be retrieved by an abusive partner. Additionally, a location tracking device (GPS) can be placed on your car or in your purse. Consider purchasing a pay as you go phone that you keep in a safe place to allow you to make calls.

Social Media

Only post things you want the public to see or know. Once it's online, it's no longer under your control. Be protective of your personal information. Your phone numbers and addresses enable people to contact you directly, and things like your birth date, the schools you attended, your employer and photos with landmarks may make it easier for someone to find where you live, hang out or go to school.

Set boundaries and limits. Tell people not to post personal information, negative comments or check-ins about you on social media. Ask people not to post or tag pictures if you're not comfortable with it.

Keep your passwords private – there is no need to share passwords to social media accounts with anyone.

If you have a friend in an abusive relationship, DO NOT post information about them without getting their permission. You could jeopardize their safety.

Courtesy The National Domestic Violence Hotline 1-800-799-7233

Works Cited

1. King, Jeanne. "Abusive Relationships - What Is the Difference between Being Abusive and Being an Abuser?" Prevent Abusive Relationships. www.preventabusiverelationships.com/dv_abusive_vs_abuser.html (accessed December 2015).

2. Bancroft, Lundy. *Why Does He Do That? Inside the Minds of Angry and Controlling Men.* New York: Berkley Books, 2003.

3. Bancroft, Lundy. "Understanding & Breaking Free From Relationship Violence - Chat Transcript" Pandora's Project. www.pandys.org/lundybancroft-transcript.html (accessed December 2015)

4. Barnes, Albert. "Commentary on Matthew 7" Study Light. www.studylight.org/commentaries/bnb/view.cgi?bk=39&ch=7. 1870 (accessed December 2015)

5. Barnes, Albert. "Commentary on Galatians 5" Study Light. www.studylight.org/commentaries/bnb/view.cgi?bk=47&ch=5. 1870 (accessed December 2015)

6. Curtis, David. "Judge Not!" Berean Bible Church. www.bereanbiblechurch.org/transcripts/matthew/som/7_1-6.htm (accessed December 2015)

7. Crippen, Jeff. "You Cannot Drive Abuse Out of the Abuser" A Cry for Justice. http://cryingoutforjustice.com/2015/11/11/you-cannot-drive-abuse-out-of-the-abuser/ (accessed December 2015)

8. University of St. Thomas. "Biblical Exegesis: 2. Examine the Historical, Cultural, and Literary Background" http://libguides.stthomas.edu/c.php?g=88712&p=573352 (accessed December 2015)

9. Butt, Kyle. "The Biblical View of Women" Apologetics Press. www.apologeticspress.org/APContent.aspx?category=13&article=3654 (accessed December 2015)

10. Fortune, Marie. *Keeping the Faith: Questions and Answers for the Abused Woman.* New York: Harper Collins Publishers, 1987.

11. Tracy, Steven. "What Does 'Submit in Everything' Really Mean? The Nature and Scope of Marital Submission" Christians for Biblical Equality. www.cbe.org.au/media/docs/SubmitinEverythingTJ.pdf (accessed December 2015)

12. Vernick, Leslie. *The Emotionally Destructive Relationship: Seeing It, Stopping It, Surviving It.* Eugene: Harvest House Publishers, 2007.

13. Grady, J. Lee. "The Dark Side of Wives Submitting to Husbands" Charisma Magazine. www.charismamag.com/blogs/fire-in-my-bones/7229-the-dark-side-of-submission (accessed December 2015)

14. Kassian, Mary. "7 Misconceptions about Submission" Girls Gone Wise. www.girlsgonewise.com/7-misconceptions-about-submission/ (accessed December 2015)

15. Branson, Brenda, Paula Silva. *Violence Among Us: Ministry to Families in Crisis.* King of Prussia: Judson Press, 2007.

16. Pryde, Debi, Robert Needham. *A Biblical Perspective of What to Do when You Are Abused by Your Husband.* Newberry Springs: Iron Sharpeneth Iron Publications, 2003.

17. Crippen, Jeff. "Bow Down, Tremble, and Pay Homage!" Sermon Audio. http://media.sermonaudio.com/mediapdf/81510163171.pdf (accessed December 2015)

18. Hallock, Mark. "Part 1: God's Design for Wives" Calvary Church podcast. http://englewood.thecalvary.org/media/sermon-archive/gospel-shaped-family/?sermon_id=148 (accessed December 2015)

19. Tracy, Steven. "What does 'Submit in Everything' Really Mean? The Nature and Scope of Marital Submission" Christians for Biblical Equality. www.cbe.org.au/media/docs/SubmitinEverythingTJ.pdf (accessed December 2015)

20. Francisco, Don. "Marriage and Divorce Myth 1 - Does God Hate Divorce?" Rocky Mountain Ministries. www.rockymountainministries.org/mythbusters/17-mythbusters/56-marriage-and-divorce-myth-1-does-god-hate-divorce-marriage-and-divorce-myth-1-does-god-hate-divorce.html (accessed December 2015)

21. Gola, Stephen. *Divorce: God's Will? The Truth of Divorce and Remarriage in the Bible for Christians.* Summerville: Holy Fire Publishing, 2005.

22. Crippen, Jeff. "Marriage, Divorce, and an Ox in a Well" A Cry for Justice. http://cryingoutforjustice.com/2014/06/15/marriage-divorce-and-an-ox-in-a-well/ (accessed December 2015)

23. Fortune, Marie. *Keeping the Faith: Questions and Answers for the Abused Woman.* New York: HarperCollins, 1987.

24. Gola, Stephen. *Divorce: God's Will? The Truth of Divorce and Remarriage in the Bible for Christians.* Summerville: Holy Fire Publishing, 2005.

25. Crippen, Jeff. "How to Deal Properly With Abusers Posing as Christians" A Cry for Justice. http://cryingoutforjustice.com/2015/09/04/how-to-deal-properly-with-abusers-posing-as-christians/ (accessed December 2015)

26. Clanchy, Michael, Chris Trotter. "Infidelity - A Form of Abuse" Sanctuary for the Abused. http://abusesanctuary.blogspot.com/2006/08/infidelity-form-of-abuse-infidelity.html (accessed December 2015)

27. Crippen, Jeff. "Dealing With the Abuser Part 2" Sermon Audio. http://media.sermonaudio.com/mediapdf/111101336242.pdf (accessed December 2015)

28. Vine, W.E. "Vine's Expository of Dictionary of NT Words" Study Light. www.studylight.org/dictionaries/ved/view.cgi?n=45 (accessed December 2015)

29. Ludwig, Robi, Matt Birkbeck. *Till Death Do Us Part: Love, Marriage, and the Mind of the Killer Spouse.* Atria Books, 2006.

30. Family Violence Prevention Fund. "Predictors of Domestic Violence Homicide" National Center on Domestic and Sexual Violence. www.ncdsv.org/images/FWV_PredictorsDVHomicide_2004.pdf (accessed December 2015)

31. Crippen, Jeff. "What About Passive Abuse?" A Cry for Justice. http://cryingoutforjustice.com/2012/04/05/what-about-passive-abuse-by-jeff-crippen/ (accessed December 2015)

32. Francisco, Don. "Marriage and Divorce Myth 2 - Is Divorce a Sin?" Rocky Mountain Ministries. www.rockymountainministries.org/mythbusters/17-mythbusters/57-

marriage-and-divorce-myth-2-is-divorce-a-sin-marriage-and-divorce-myth-2-is-divorce-a-sin.html (accessed December 2015).

33. Hunt, June. "How to Respond to Verbal and Emotional Abusers" The Christian Post. www.christianpost.com/news/how-to-respond-to-verbal-emotional-abusers-78253/ (accessed December 2015).

34. Cunningham, Alison, Linda Baker. "Little Eyes, Little Ears: How Violence against a Mother Shapes Children as They Grow" London Family Court Clinic. www.lfcc.on.ca/little_eyes_little_ears.pdf (accessed December 2015).

35. Holcomb, Lindsey, Justin Holcomb. *Is It My Fault: Hope and Healing for Those Suffering Domestic Violence*. Chicago: Moody Publishers, 2014.

36. Fortune, Marie. *Keeping the Faith: Guidance for Christian Women Facing Abuse*. San Francisco: Harper One, 1995.

37. Crippen, Jeff. "Dealing With the Abuser" Sermon Audio. http://media.sermonaudio.com/mediapdf/1025101328587.pdf (accessed December 2015).

38. Fortune, Marie. *Keeping the Faith: Guidance for Christian Women Facing Abuse*. San Francisco: Harper One, 1995.

39. Heggen, Carolyn. *Sexual Abuse in Christian Homes and Churches*. Eugene: Wipf and Stock, 2006.

40. Crippen, Jeff. *A Cry for Justice: How the Evil of Domestic Abuse Hides in Your Church*. Calvary Press, 2012.

41. Kroeger, Catherine. Quote in book *Domestic Violence: What Every Pastor Needs to Know* by Al Miles. Minneapolis: Fortress Press, 2011.

42. Crippen, Jeff. "'Christian' Enabling of the Abuser Increases His Attacks on the Victim" A Cry for Justice. http://cryingoutforjustice.com/2015/11/30/christian-enabling-of-the-abuser-increases-his-attacks-on-the-victim/ (accessed December 2015)

43. Moore, Russell. "The Church and Violence Against Women" Russell Moore. www.russellmoore.com/2014/09/09/the-church-and-violence-against-women/ (accessed December 2015).

44. Adams, Carol. "When the Abuser Is Among Us: One Church's Response to a Perpetrator" Faith Trust Institute.

www.faithtrustinstitute.org/resources/articles/When-the-Abuser-Is-Among-Us.pdf (accessed December 2015)

45. Crippen, Jeff. *A Cry for Justice: How the Evil of Domestic Abuse Hides in Your Church.* Calvary Press, 2012.

46. Roberts, Barbara. "The Bible DOES allow divorce for domestic abuse" A Cry for Justice. http://cryingoutforjustice.com/2014/10/10/the-bible-does-allow-divorce-for-domestic-abuse/ (accessed December 2015)

47. The Mama Bear Effect. "Putting Child Safety First" http://themamabeareffect.org/putting-child-safety-first.html (accessed December 2015)

48. Bancroft, Lundy. "Understanding and Breaking Free From Relationship Violence - Chat Transcript" Pandora's Project. www.pandys.org/lundybancroft-transcript.html (accessed December 2015)

49. Vernick, Leslie. "Can I Divorce My Abusive Spouse?" Leslie Vernick. http://leslievernick.com/can-i-divorce-my-abusive-spouse/ (accessed December 2015)

50. Bancroft, Lundy. "Understanding and Breaking Free From Relationship Violence - Chat Transcript" Pandora's Project. www.pandys.org/lundybancroft-transcript.html (accessed December 2015)

51. Bancroft, Lundy. "Understanding and Breaking Free From Relationship Violence - Chat Transcript" Pandora's Project. www.pandys.org/lundybancroft-transcript.html (accessed December 2015)

52. Crippen, Jeff. "No Abuser is Hidden From His Sight" Sermon Audio. http://media.sermonaudio.com/mediapdf/1012101540520.pdf (accessed December 2015)

53. Women's Resource Service. "Grief and Loss after Abuse"

54. Fortune, Marie. *Keeping the Faith: Questions and Answers for the Abused Woman.* New York: Harper Collins, 1987.

Resources

Helplines (accessed January 2016)

National Domestic Violence Hotline 1-800-799-7233 www.thehotline.org/

Americans Overseas Domestic Violence (and sexual assault support) Crisis Center 1-866-USWOMEN www.866uswomen.org/

Love is Respect (empowering youth to end dating abuse) 1-866-331-9474 www.loveisrespect.org/

Men's Domestic Abuse Helpline 1-800-HELPLINE http://dahmw.org/

National Center for Elder Abuse 1-855-500-3537 www.ncea.aoa.gov/

National Center for Victims of Crime 1-202-467-8700 www.victimsofcrime.org/

National Child Abuse Hotline 1-800-422-4453 www.childhelp.org/

National Clearinghouse for the Defense of Battered Women 1-800-903-0111 x 3 www.ncdbw.org/

National Coalition against Domestic Violence 1-800-799-SAFE www.ncadv.org/

National Coalition for the Homeless 1-202-737-6444 www.nationalhomeless.org/

National Suicide Prevention Lifeline 1-800-273-8255 www.suicidepreventionlifeline.org/

RAINN (Rape, Abuse and Incest National Network) 1-800-656-HOPE https://rainn.org/index.php

Websites (accessed January 2016)

Womens Law www.womenslaw.org/

Pandora's Project (support and resources for survivors of rape and sexual abuse) www.pandys.org/index.html

Bursting the Bubble (support for teens and young adults about domestic violence) www.burstingthebubble.com/

Domestic Shelters (find a domestic violence help and shelter near you) www.domesticshelters.org/

RAVE (Religion and Violence e-Learning) www.theraveproject.com/index.php

Custody Preparation for Moms (support for moms by those who have been through it) www.custodyprepformoms.org/pas.htm

GRACE Godly Response to Abuse in the Christian Environment (empowering the Christian community to recognize and respond to the sin of child abuse) www.netgrace.org/

Courageous Kids Network (support for young people) www.courageouskids.net/

Protective Parent Storehouse https://sites.google.com/a/oakland.edu/protective-parent-storehouse/home (If you are a protective/non-offending parent involved in a custody dispute where a potential abuser, his/her legal team, or Child Protective Services (CPS) has accused you of false reporting or characterized you as vengeful and mentally ill (Parental Alienation Syndrome, Munchausen by Proxy, etc.)

Protective Mothers' Alliance International http://protectivemothersallianceinternational.org/

Children against Court Appointed Child Abuse (support when children are legally forced to have contact with the abuser or alienated from their protective parent) http://ca3cacaca.blogspot.com/

Manipulative People www.manipulative-people.com/

Safe-at-last's Survival Guide For Victims Of Family Violence & Domestic Abuse http://hubpages.com/relationships/Domestic-Violence-OK-So-its-Abuse-What-Now

BIFF Response (respond to hostile emails, texts and other communications) www.biffresponse.com/

The Cycle of Abuse Wheel
http://storage.cloversites.com/abuserecoveryministryservices/documents/abuse%20cycle_2.pdf

Lundy Bancroft www.lundybancroft.com/
http://lundybancroft.blogspot.com/

Prevent Abusive Relationships www.preventabusiverelationships.com/index.php

Focus Ministries (Faith Based DV Help for Women and Families) www.focusministries1.org/

Leslie Vernick http://leslievernick.com/

The Mordecai Project www.themordecaiproject.org/welcome/

Girls Gone Wise www.girlsgonewise.com/

Don Francisco www.rockymountainministries.org/

Faith Trust Institute www.faithtrustinstitute.org/

A Cry for Justice http://cryingoutforjustice.com/

Sanctuary for the Abused http://abusesanctuary.blogspot.com/

The Mama Bear Effect http://themamabeareffect.org/

Articles (accessed January 2016)

"Assessing Risk to Children from Batterers" by Lundy Bancroft www.lundybancroft.com/

"The Batterer as Parent" by Lundy Bancroft www.lundybancroft.com/

"Understanding the Batterer in Custody and Visitation Disputes" by Lundy Bancroft www.lundybancroft.com/

"Safety Planning with Children of Battered Women" by Lundy Bancroft www.lundybancroft.com/

"The Connection between Batterers and Child Sexual Abuse Perpetrators" by Lundy Bancroft www.lundybancroft.com/

"Honouring Resistance: How Women Resist Abuse in Intimate Relationships" pdf by Calgary Women's Shelter www.calgarywomensshelter.com/images/pdf/cwesResistancebookletfinalweb.pdf

"Expecting Magic from Abuser Programs" by Lundy Bancroft http://lundybancroft.blogspot.com.au/

"Contrition, Behavior and Therapy" by Dr. Simon www.manipulative-people.com/

"Resistance to Violence: A Key Symptom of Chronic Mental Wellness" pdf by Martine Renoux and Allan Wade www.valdinararelationer.se/

"Assessing Dangerousness in Men Who Abuse Women" by Lundy Bancroft www.lundybancroft.com/

"Toxic Relationship Aftermath: Doubt, Mistrust and Paranoia" by Dr. Simon www.manipulative-people.com/

"What's the Difference between Normal Marital Conflict and Abuse?" by Jeff Olson http://questions.org/

"Divorced is NOT a Status" by Joseph Pote http://josephjpote.com/

"Does 1 Corinthians 7:10-11 Mean a Victim of Abuse Can't Remarry?" by Barbara Roberts http://notunderbondage.blogspot.com.au/

Recommended Books

A Cry for Justice: How the Evil of Domestic Abuse Hides in Your Church by Jeff Crippen

Not Under Bondage: Biblical Divorce for Abuse, Adultery and Desertion by Barbara Roberts

Why Does He Do That? Inside the Minds of Angry and Controlling Men by Lundy Bancroft

Should I Stay or Should I Go? A Guide to Knowing if your Relationship Can - and Should - be Saved by Lundy Bancroft

Unholy Charade: Unmasking the Domestic Abuser in the Church by Jeff Crippen with Rebecca Davis

In Sheep's Clothing: Understanding and Dealing with Manipulative People by George Simon, Jr

The Sociopath Next Door by Martha Stout

Keeping the Faith: Questions and Answers for the Abused Woman by Marie Fortune

The Emotionally Destructive Relationship: Seeing It, Stopping It, Surviving It by Leslie Vernick

Violence Among Us: Ministry to Families in Crisis by Brenda Branson and Paula Silva

A Biblical Perspective of What to Do when You Are Abused by Your Husband by Debi Pryde and Robert Needham

Divorce: God's Will? The Truth of Divorce and Remarriage in the Bible for Christians by Stephen Gola

'Till Death Do Us Part: Love, Marriage, and the Mind of the Killer Spouse by Robi Ludwig and Matt Birbeck

Is It My Fault: Hope and Healing for Those Suffering Domestic Violence by Lindsey Holcomb and Justin Holcomb

Keeping the Faith: Guidance for Christian Women Facing Abuse by Marie Fortune

Sexual Abuse in Christian Homes and Churches by Carolyn Heggen

About the Author

Robin Mullins Senger is a certified Relationship Crisis Life Coach, inspirational writer, and speaker. Raised in the Oregon Outback, she now enjoys living and recreating with her family in the Colorado Rockies.

Connect with Robin

I really appreciate you reading my book! Here are my social media coordinates:

Like me on Facebook: www.facebook.com/butterfootlife

Connect on LinkedIn: www.linkedin.com/in/robinmullinssenger

Follow me on Google+: https:/plus.google.com/+RobinMullinsSenger411

Watch me on YouTube: www.youtube.com/c/RobinMullinsSenger411

Visit my website: www.butterfootlife.com

Supporting, guiding and empowering women, men and teens in a relationship crisis.

If you are a church or school, contact me about domestic violence training for your staff, or hosting a workshop for youth and dating violence prevention.